TEACHING LITTLE FINGERS TO PLAY
SONGBOOK

Original Piano Solos and Arrangements
with Optional Teacher Accompaniments by

Glenda Austin

Eric Baumgartner

Randall Hartsell

Carolyn Miller

Mary K. Sallee

and

Carolyn C. Setliff

Cover Illustrations by Nick Gressle

PLAYBACK+
Speed · Pitch · Balance · Loop

To access audio, visit:
www.halleonard.com/mylibrary

Enter Code
"3760-8405-4552-8028"

ISBN 978-1-4234-6970-4

EXCLUSIVELY DISTRIBUTED BY

WILLIS MUSIC

HAL•LEONARD®

Visit Hal Leonard Online at
www.halleonard.com

Contact us:
Hal Leonard
7777 West Bluemound Road
Milwaukee, WI 53213
Email: info@halleonard.com

In Europe, contact:
Hal Leonard Europe Limited
42 Wigmore Street
Marylebone, London, W1U 2RN
Email: info@halleonardeurope.com

In Australia, contact:
Hal Leonard Australia Pty. Ltd.
4 Lentara Court
Cheltenham, Victoria, 3192 Australia
Email: info@halleonard.com.au

CONTENTS

Hint!—
Ad lib. is short for *ad libitum,* which is Latin for "at will." When you have mastered the piece, try improvising some of the notes or tempo.

Student Position
One octave higher when performing as a duet

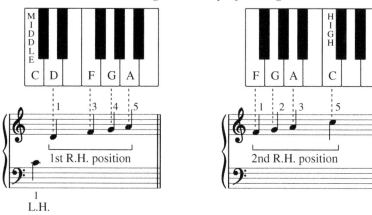

Amazing Grace
Optional Teacher Accompaniment

Words by John Newton
From *A Collection of Sacred Ballads*
Traditional American Melody
From Carrell and Clayton's *Virginia Harmony*
Arranged by Edwin O. Excell
Adapted by Mary K. Sallee

Moderately

mf

With pedal

Repeat ad lib.

Amazing Grace

Words by John Newton
From *A Collection of Sacred Ballads*
Traditional American Melody
From Carrell and Clayton's *Virginia Harmony*
Arranged by Edwin O. Excell
Adapted by Mary K. Sallee

Play both hands one octave higher when performing as a duet.

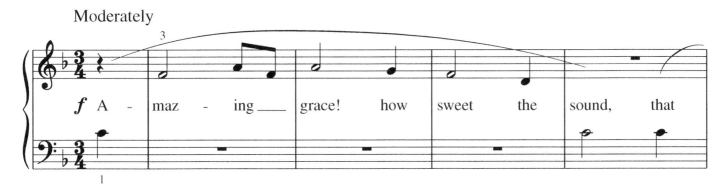

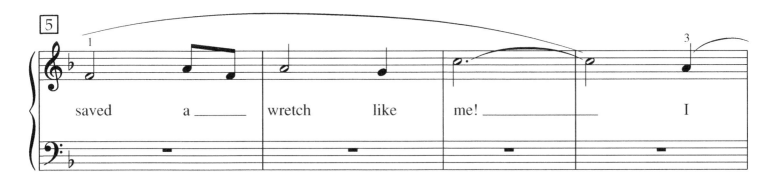

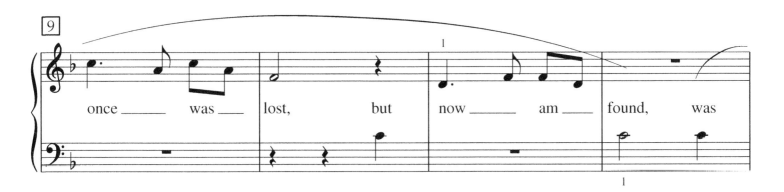

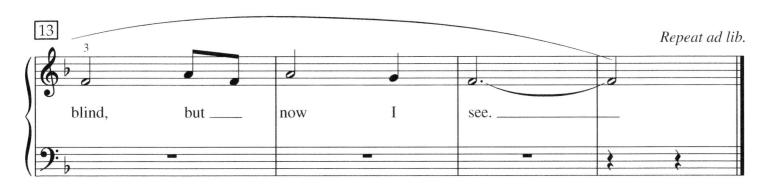

6

Student Position
One octave higher when performing as a duet

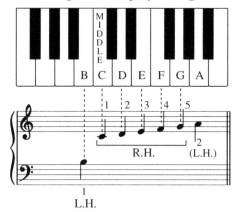

America
(My Country, 'Tis of Thee)
Optional Teacher Accompaniment

Words by Samuel Francis Smith
Music from *Thesaurus Musicus*
Arranged by Eric Baumgartner

America
(My Country, 'Tis of Thee)

Words by Samuel Francis Smith
Music from *Thesaurus Musicus*
Arranged by Eric Baumgartner

Play both hands one octave higher when performing as a duet.

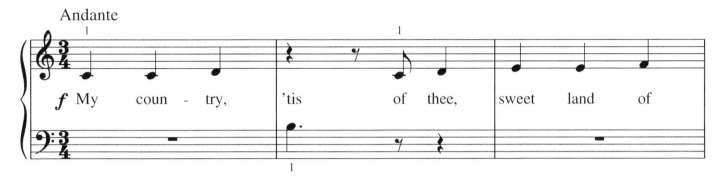

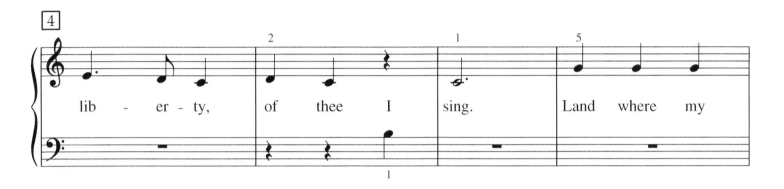

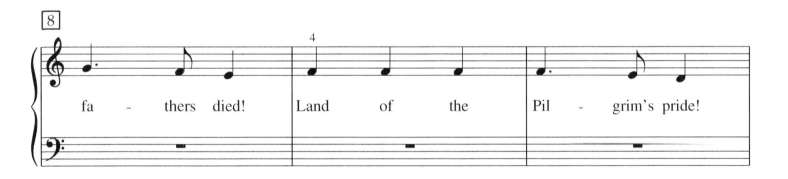

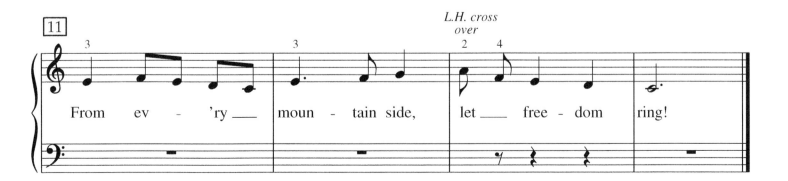

Did You Know?—
This song began as a poem written by Katherine Lee Bates in 1895. Many composers have set these moving words to music. This version, the best-known melody, was taken from a hymn composed by Samuel A. Ward.

Student Position

One octave higher when performing as a duet

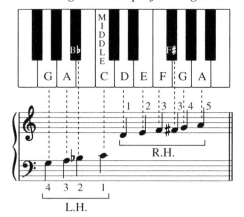

America, the Beautiful

Optional Teacher Accompaniment

Words by Katherine Lee Bates
Music by Samuel A. Ward
Arranged by Eric Baumgartner

America, the Beautiful

Words by Katherine Lee Bates
Music by Samuel A. Ward
Arranged by Eric Baumgartner

Play both hands one octave higher when performing as a duet.

Majestically

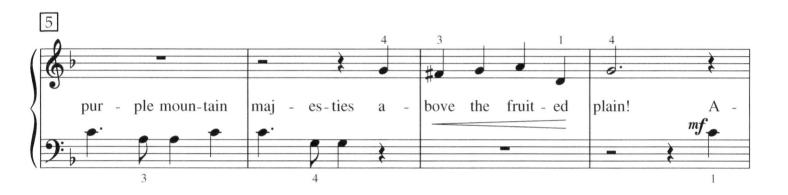

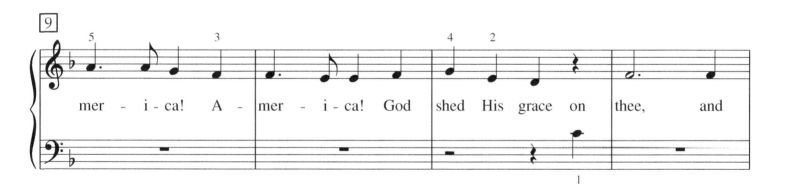

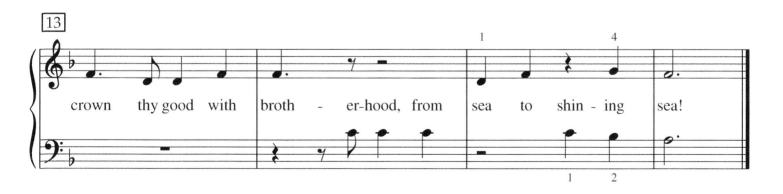

Hint!—
Practice the left hand in measures 9-13
several times until it becomes comfortable.

Did You Know?—
There is also a popular Elvis Presley song
that uses this melody. Perhaps you've heard
of it: "Love Me Tender."

Aura Lee
Optional Teacher Accompaniment

Words by W.W. Fosdick
Music by George R. Poulton
Arranged by Glenda Austin

Aura Lee

Words by W.W. Fosdick
Music by George R. Poulton
Arranged by Glenda Austin

Play both hands one octave higher when performing as a duet.

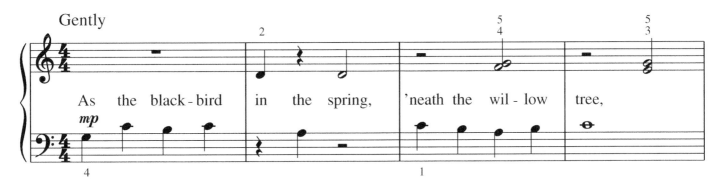

As the black-bird in the spring, 'neath the wil-low tree,

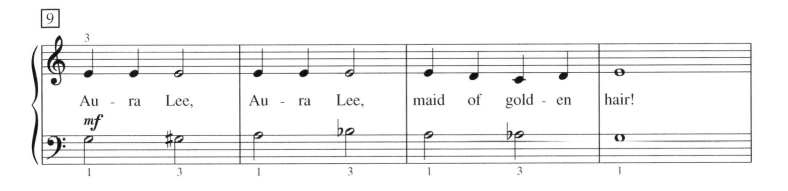

sat and piped, I heard him sing, sing-ing "Au - ra Lee!"

Au - ra Lee, Au - ra Lee, maid of gold - en hair!

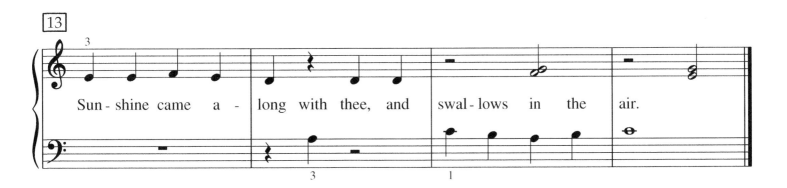

Sun - shine came a - long with thee, and swal - lows in the air.

STEPHEN FOSTER was the first great American songwriter. He wrote over 200 songs, including "Beautiful Dreamer," back in the 1800s. Many of his songs are still loved and performed today, over a century later!

Prepare!—
The 4th finger in each hand plays a black note. Before playing, prepare finger 4 on G-sharp (L.H.) and on F-sharp (R.H.).

Student Position
One octave higher when performing as a duet

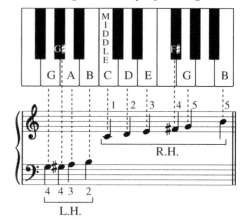

Beautiful Dreamer
Optional Teacher Accompaniment

Words and Music by
Stephen C. Foster (1826–1864)
Arranged by Carolyn C. Setliff

Beautiful Dreamer

Words and Music by
Stephen C. Foster (1826–1864)
Arranged by Carolyn C. Setliff

Play both hands one octave higher when performing as a duet.

Expressively

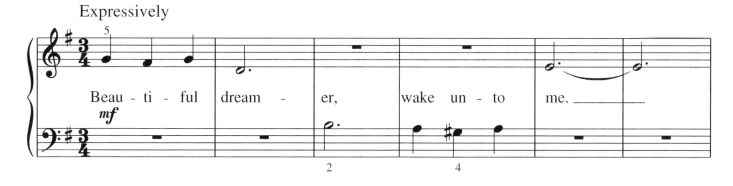

Beau - ti - ful dream - er, wake un - to me. _____

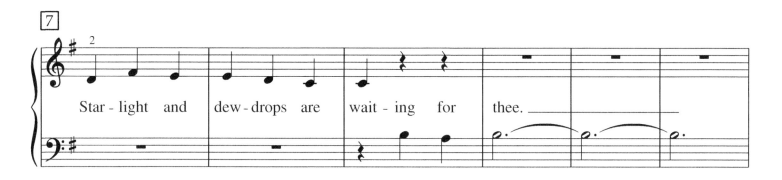

Star - light and dew-drops are wait - ing for thee. _____

Sounds of the rude world heard in the day, _____

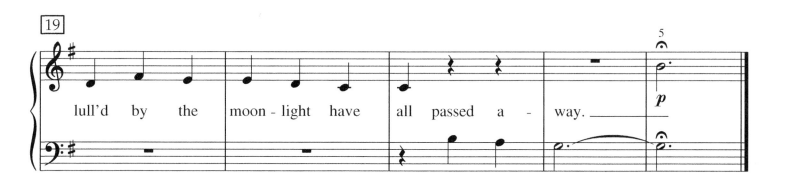

lull'd by the moon - light have all passed a - way. _____

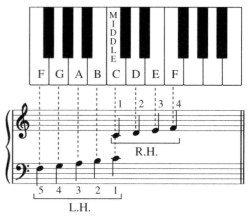

Student Position
One octave higher when performing as a duet

Bingo
Optional Teacher Accompaniment

Traditional
Arranged by Glenda Austin

With spirit

mf

Bingo

Traditional
Arranged by Glenda Austin

Play both hands one octave higher when performing as a duet.

With spirit

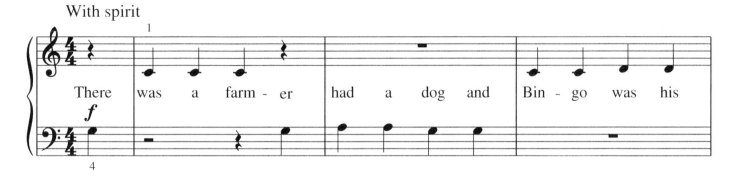

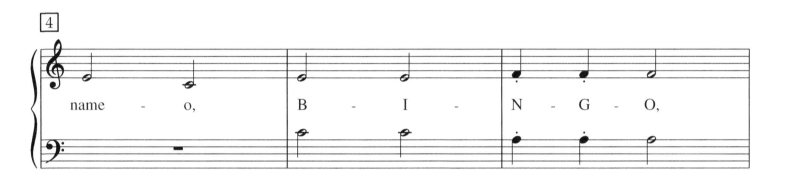

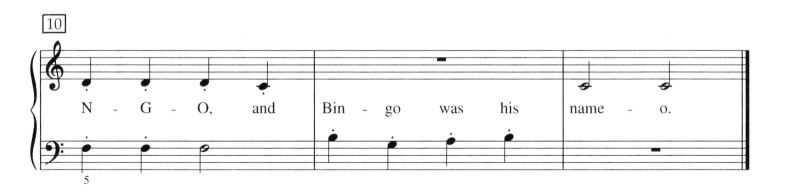

16

Student Position
One octave higher when performing as a duet

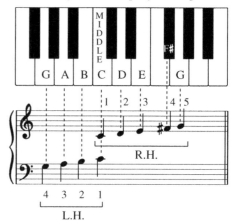

Buffalo Gals
Optional Teacher Accompaniment

Words and Music by Cool White (John Hodges)
Arranged by Glenda Austin

Leisurely

Buffalo Gals

Words and Music by Cool White (John Hodges)
Arranged by Glenda Austin

Play both hands one octave higher when performing as a duet.

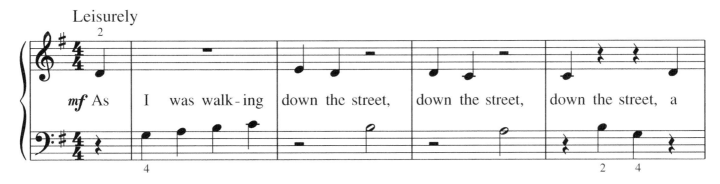

18

Did You Know?—
This song was written by Brigadier General Edmund L. Gruber when he was a first lieutenant stationed in the Philippines in 1908. *Caissons* were horse-drawn vehicles that carried ammunition. The words to this song were updated after World War II, and it is now also known as "The Army Song."

Student Position
One octave higher when performing as a duet

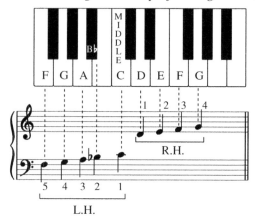

The Caissons Go Rolling Along
Optional Teacher Accompaniment

Words and Music by Edmund L. Gruber
Arranged by Eric Baumgartner

The Caissons Go Rolling Along

Words and Music by Edmund L. Gruber
Arranged by Eric Baumgartner

Play both hands one octave higher when performing as a duet.

Boldly

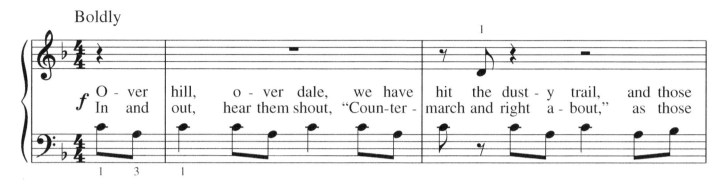

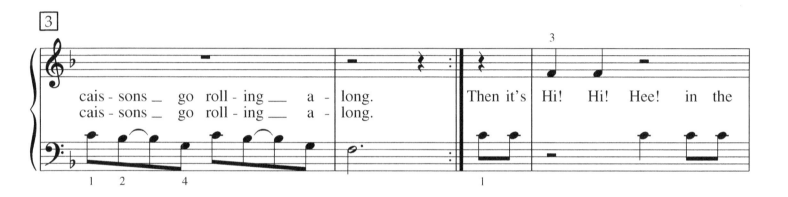

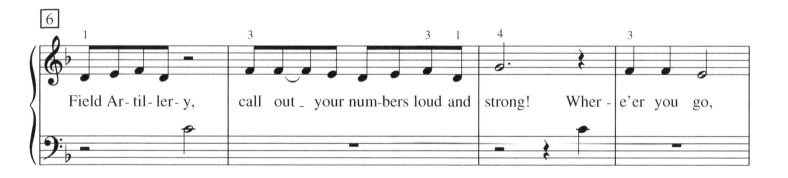

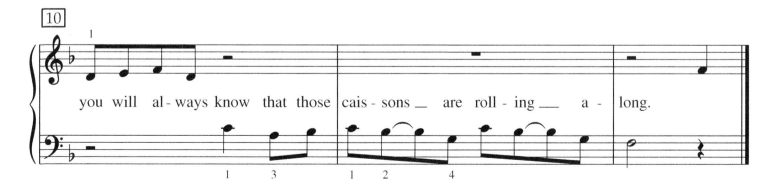

Did You Know?—
Orpheus in the Underworld is an operetta (light opera) by French composer Jacques Offenbach. The "Can-Can" is actually taken from the most famous number in the opera, the *Galop Infernal*.

Hint!—
Allegro means "cheerful" in Italian. Pieces marked *allegro* are played fast and lively.

Student Position
One octave higher when performing as a duet

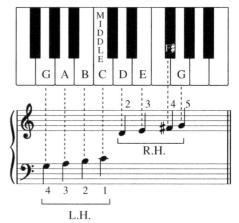

Can-Can
from *Orpheus in the Underworld*

Optional Teacher Accompaniment

Jacques Offenbach (1819–1880)
Arranged by Randall Hartsell

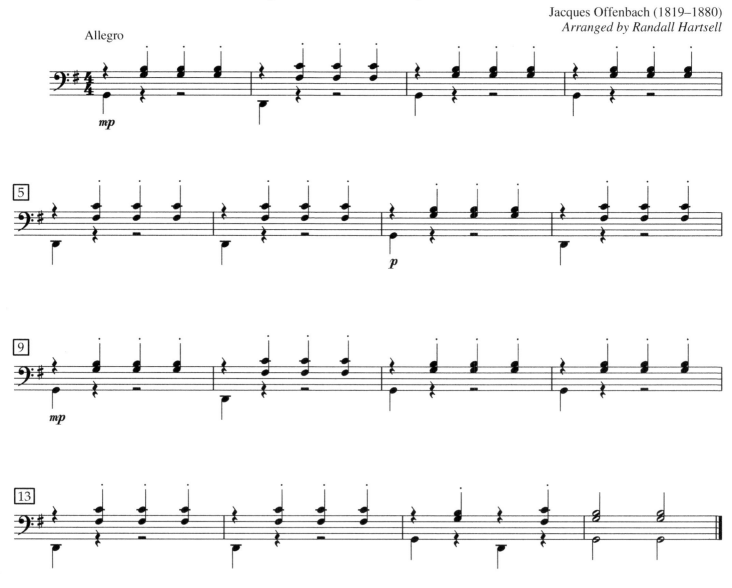

Can-Can
from *Orpheus in the Underworld*

Jacques Offenbach (1819-1880)
Arranged by Randall Hartsell

Play both hands one octave higher when performing as a duet.

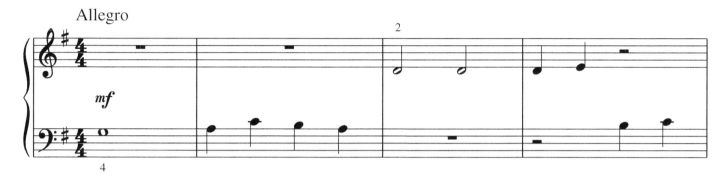

22

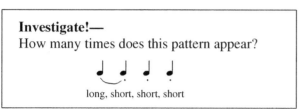

Investigate!—
How many times does this pattern appear?

long, short, short, short

Student Position
One octave higher when performing as a duet

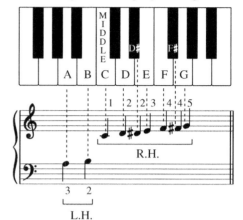

Caravan
Optional Teacher Accompaniment

Carolyn Miller

Caravan

Carolyn Miller

Play both hands one octave higher when performing as a duet.

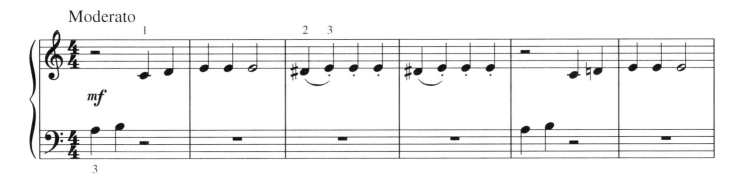

Cielito Lindo (Little Pretty Sky)—
This catchy tune begs to be played and sung out loud!
(Try it.) The song gained popularity during the
Mexican Revolution of the early 20th century and
is now recognized around the world. It is often
performed with strumming guitars.

Student Position
One octave higher when performing as a duet

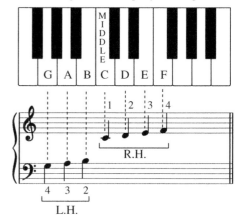

Cielito Lindo
Optional Teacher Accompaniment

C. Fernandez
Arranged by Carolyn C. Setliff

Cielito Lindo

C. Fernandez
Arranged by Carolyn C. Setliff

Play both hands one octave higher when performing as a duet.

Cheerfully

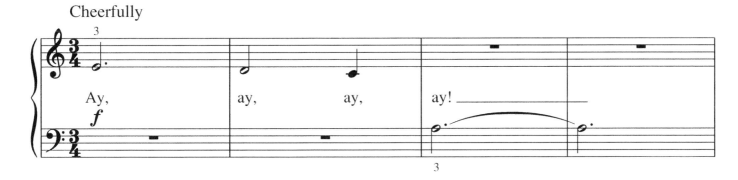

Ay,   ay,   ay,   ay!

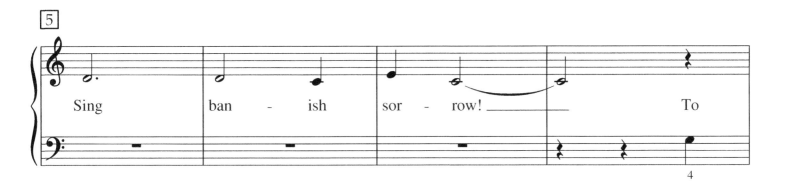

Sing   ban - ish   sor - row! _____   To

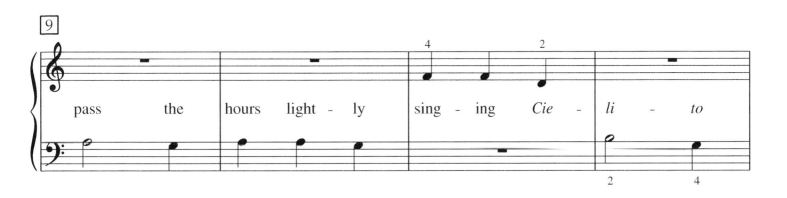

pass   the   hours   light - ly   sing - ing   *Cie* -   *li* -   *to*

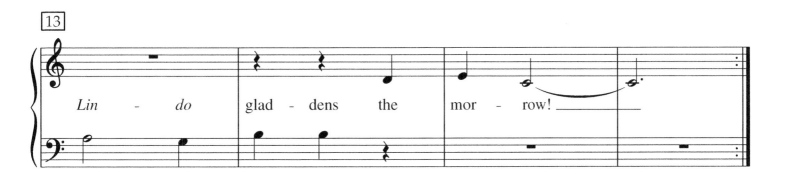

Lin -   *do*   glad - dens   the   mor - row! _____

Student Position

One octave higher when performing as a duet

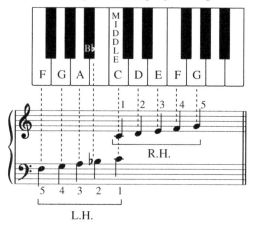

Country Gardens
Optional Teacher Accompaniment

Traditional
Arranged by Randall Hartsell

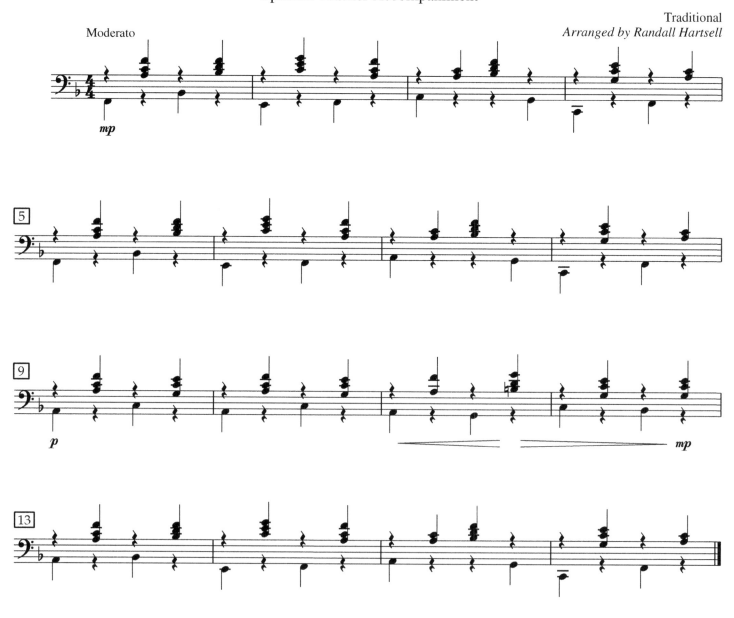

Country Gardens

Traditional
Arranged by Randall Hartsell

Play both hands one octave higher when performing as a duet.

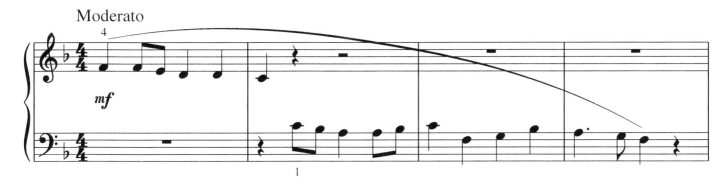

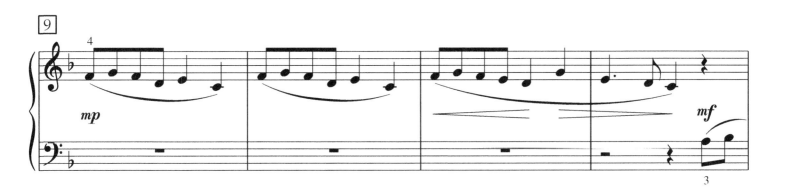

Hint!—
Try to always get the "pinky" (5th finger) to play on the fingertip.

Remember—a natural (♮) cancels a sharp (♯). How many measures have both an F♯ and an F♮?

Student Position

One octave higher when performing as a duet

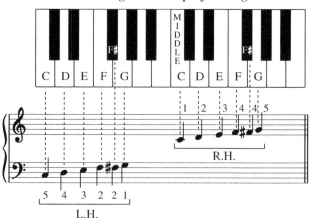

The Dancing Puppet
Optional Teacher Accompaniment

Carolyn Miller

The Dancing Puppet

Carolyn Miller

Play both hands one octave higher when performing as a duet.

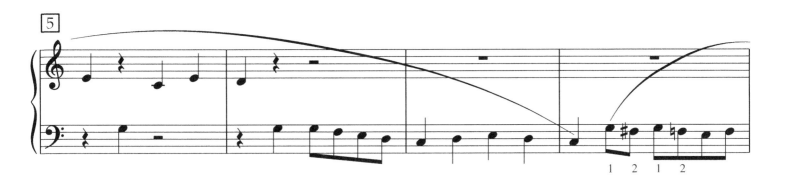

Reminder—
When you see *ritardando* (*ritard.* or
rit. for short.) in a piece of music, it means
to gradually slow down.

Student Position
One octave higher when performing as a duet

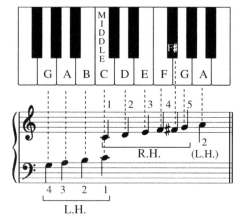

Deck the Hall
Optional Teacher Accompaniment

Traditional Welsh Carol
Arranged by Carolyn Miller

Happily

mf

rit.

Deck the Hall

Traditional Welsh Carol
Arranged by Carolyn Miller

Play both hands one octave higher when performing as a duet.

Happily

Deck the hall with boughs of hol - ly, Fa la la la la, la la la la.

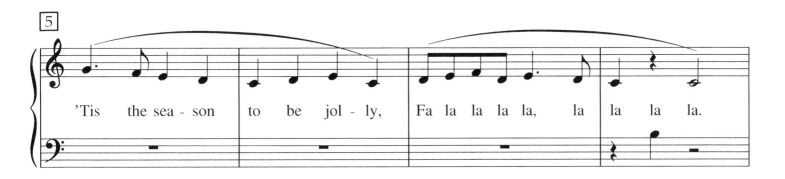

'Tis the sea - son to be jol - ly, Fa la la la la, la la la la.

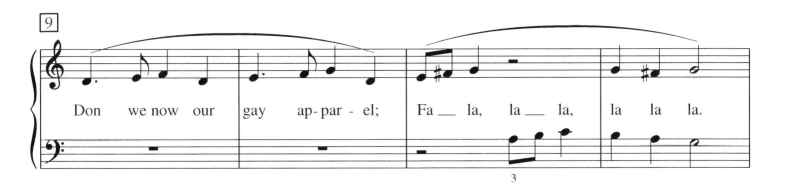

Don we now our gay ap-par-el; Fa __ la, la __ la, la la la.

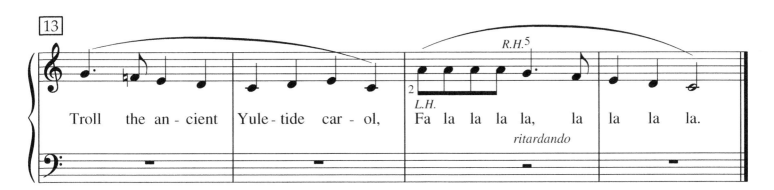

Troll the an - cient Yule - tide car - ol, Fa la la la la, la la la la.

ritardando

Doo Wop at the Sock Hop

Eric Baumgartner

Play as written when performing as a duet.

50's style Rock

snap fingers or slap thigh

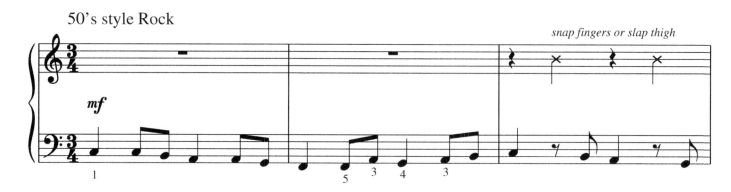

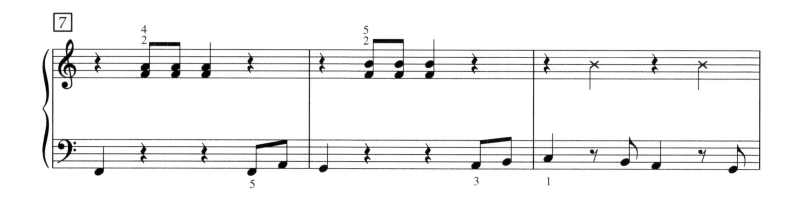

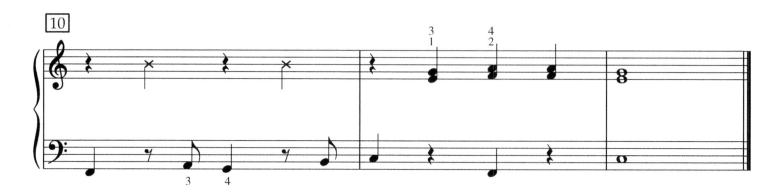

Reminder!—

In music notation there are signs of silence called *rests*, which tell us when and for how long our fingers should be silent.

Quarter Rest   𝄽   = 1 count

Half Rest   ▬   = 2 counts

Whole Rest*   ▬   = 4 counts

Eighth Rest   𝄾   = 1/2 count

*The WHOLE REST receives the counts for the whole measure indicated by the top number of the time signature.

Student Position

Play as written when performing as a duet

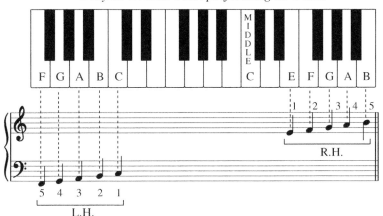

Doo Wop at the Sock Hop

Optional Teacher Accompaniment

Eric Baumgartner

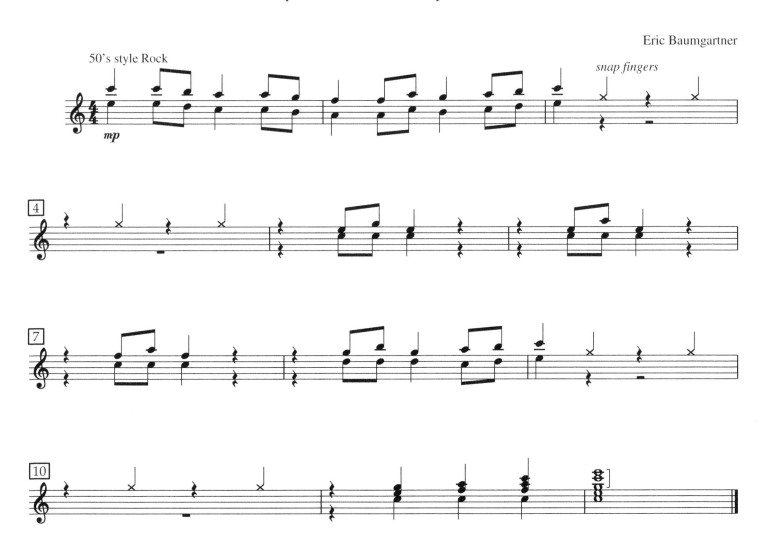

Student Position

One octave higher when performing as a duet

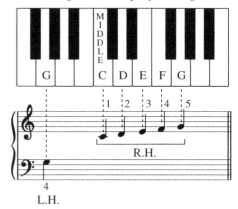

Down at the Station
Optional Teacher Accompaniment

Traditional
Arranged by Glenda Austin

Steadily

mf

5

9

13

Down at the Station

Traditional
Arranged by Glenda Austin

Play both hands one octave higher when performing as a duet.

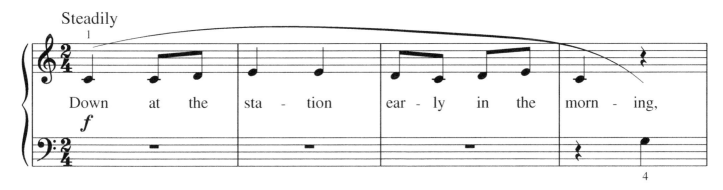

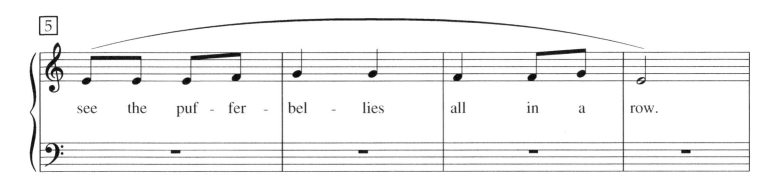

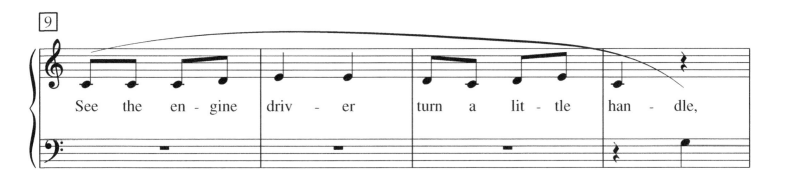

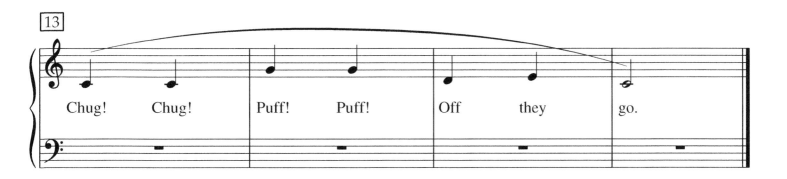

Student Position
One octave higher when performing as a duet

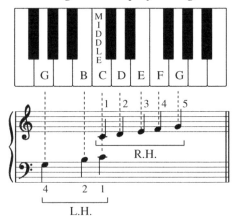

Down in the Valley
Optional Teacher Accompaniment

Traditional American Folk Song
Arranged by Glenda Austin

Flowing

mp

7

13

19

Down in the Valley

Traditional American Folk Song
Arranged by Glenda Austin

Play both hands one octave higher when performing as a duet.

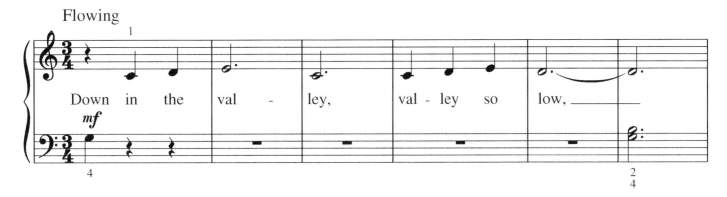

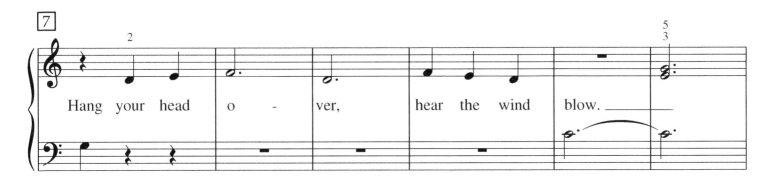

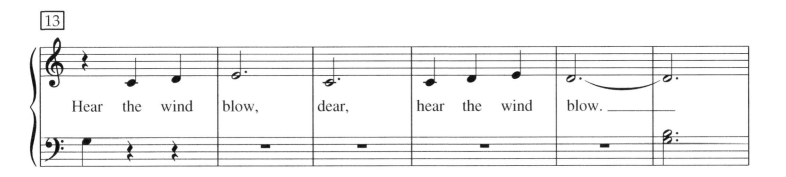

Student Position

One octave higher when performing as a duet

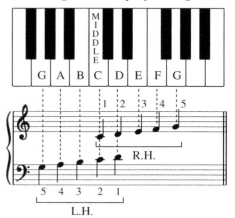

For the Beauty of the Earth
Optional Teacher Accompaniment

Words by Folliot S. Pierpoint
Music by Conrad Kocher
Arranged by Mary K. Sallee

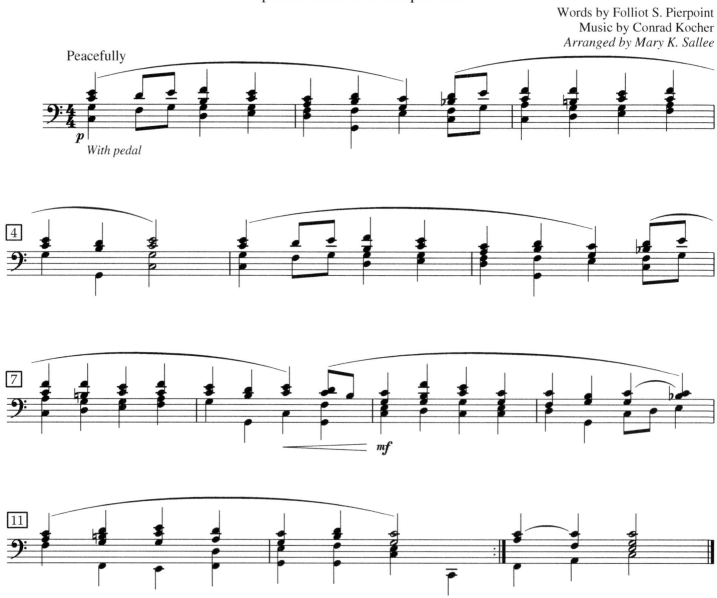

For the Beauty of the Earth

Words by Folliot S. Pierpoint
Music by Conrad Kocher
Arranged by Mary K. Sallee

Play both hands one octave higher when performing as a duet.

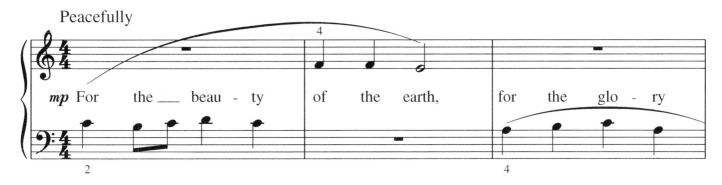

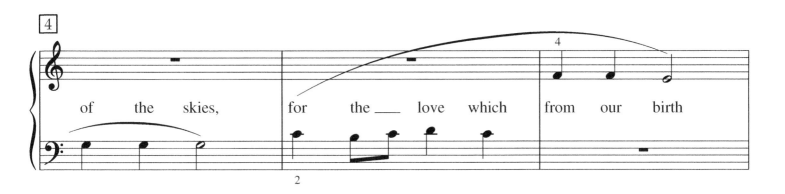

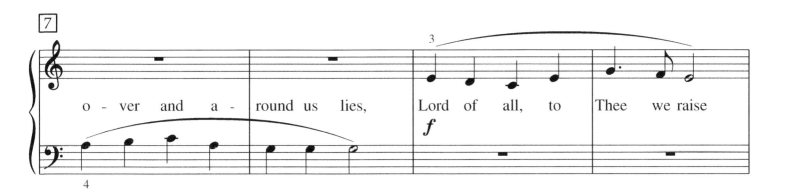

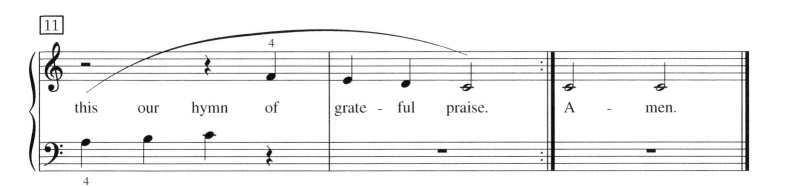

40

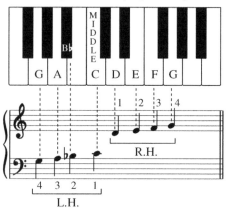
A Groovy Tune
Optional Teacher Accompaniment

Eric Baumgartner

Moderately fast

mf

A Groovy Tune

Eric Baumgartner

Play both hands one octave higher when performing as a duet.

Moderately fast

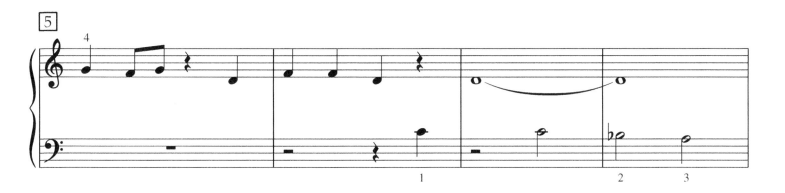

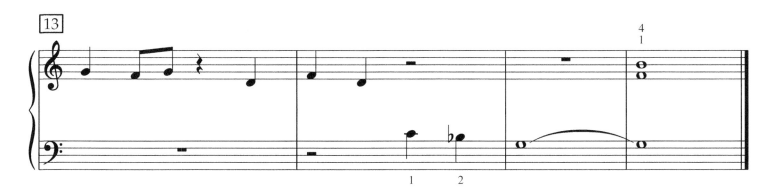

Did You Know?—
The national anthem of Israel was written in 1878 and published in 1886 as a poem. It was adopted as the official Zionist anthem in 1933, fifteen years before the State of Israel was born.

English:
As long as a Jewish spirit yearns deep in the heart,
With eyes turned toward the East, looking
    toward Zion,
Then our hope will not be lost, the hope of
    two thousand years:
To be a free people in our own land,
The land of Zion and Jerusalem.

Student Position
One octave higher when performing as a duet

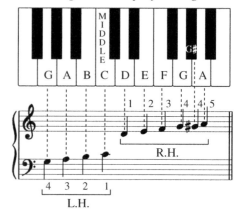

Hatikvah
Optional Teacher Accompaniment

Traditional Hebrew Melody
Lyrics by N.H. Imber
Arranged by Eric Baumgartner

Hatikvah

Traditional Hebrew Melody
Lyrics by N.H. Imber
Arranged by Eric Baumgartner

Play both hands one octave higher when performing as a duet.

With dignity

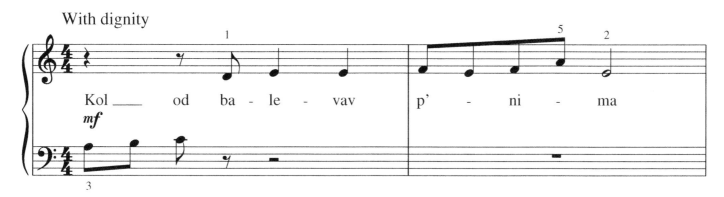

Kol ___ od ba - le - vav p' - ni - ma

ne - fesh y' - hu - di ho - mi - ya, ul' - fa - a - te ___ miz - rach

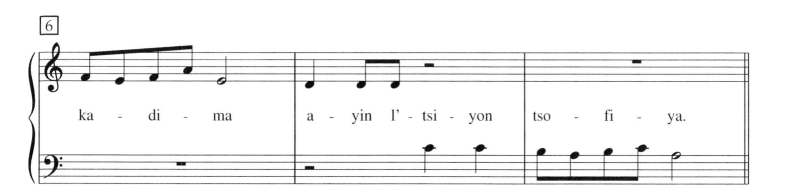

ka - di - ma a - yin l' - tsi - yon tso - fi - ya.

44

Optional Teacher Accompaniment

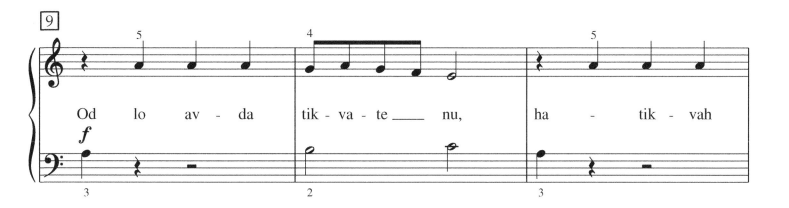

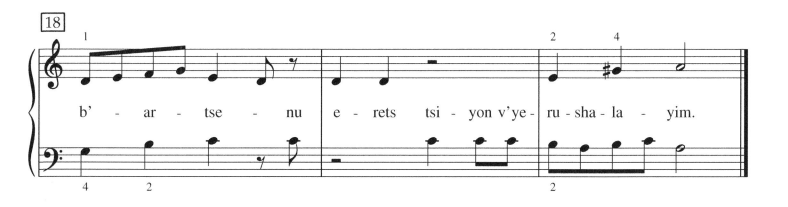

46

English:
We wish peace upon you.

Note:
"Ch" is pronounced as a guttural "h" sound.

Student Position
One octave higher when performing as a duet

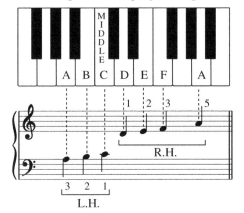

Heyveynu Shalom Aleichem
Optional Teacher Accompaniment

Traditional Hebrew
Arranged by Eric Baumgartner

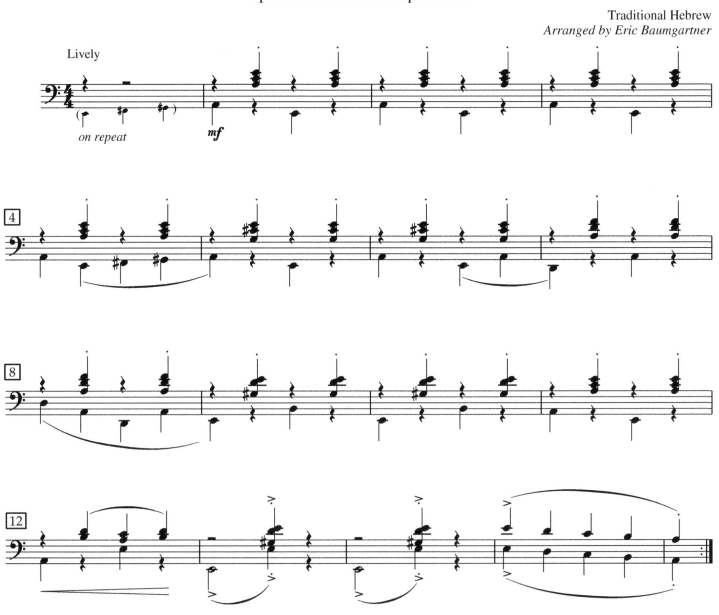

Heyveynu Shalom Aleichem

Traditional Hebrew
Arranged by Eric Baumgartner

Play both hands one octave higher when performing as a duet.

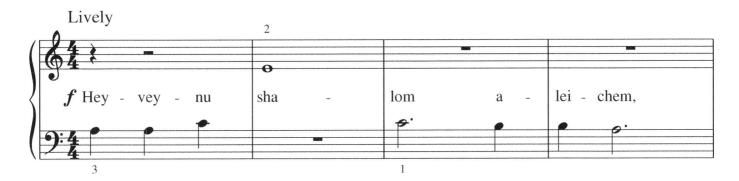

Hey - vey - nu sha - lom a - lei - chem,

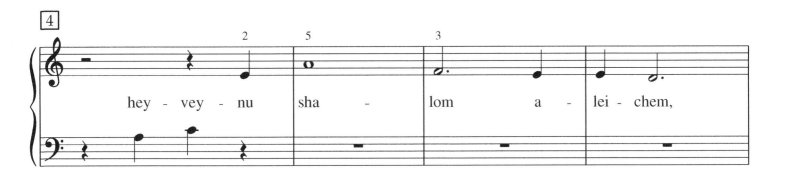

hey - vey - nu sha - lom a - lei - chem,

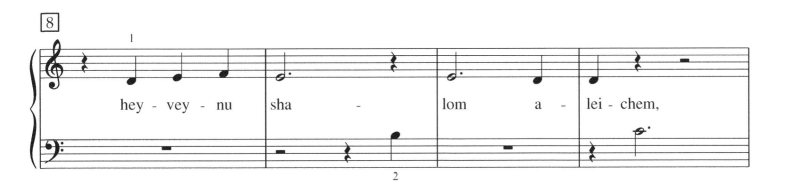

hey - vey - nu sha - lom a - lei - chem,

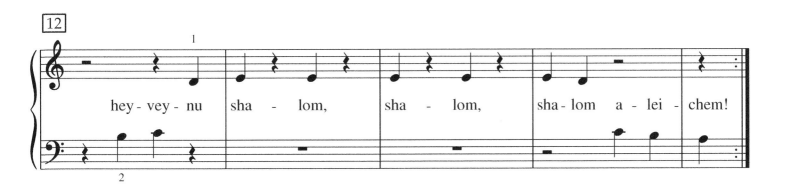

hey - vey - nu sha - lom, sha - lom, sha - lom a - lei - chem!

Student Position

One octave higher when performing as a duet

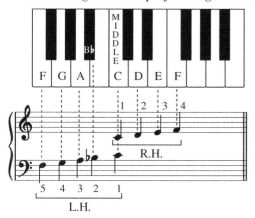

Holy, Holy, Holy
Optional Teacher Accompaniment

Words by Reginald Heber
Music by John B. Dykes
Arranged by Mary K. Sallee

Holy, Holy, Holy

Words by Reginald Heber
Music by John B. Dykes
Arranged by Mary K. Sallee

Play both hands one octave higher when performing as a duet.

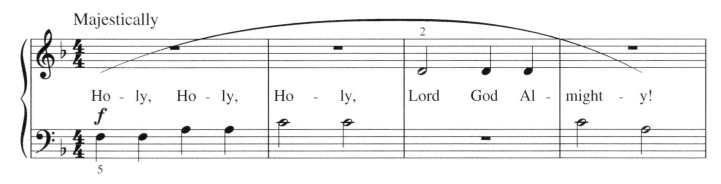

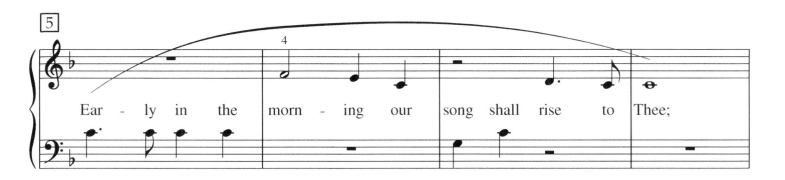

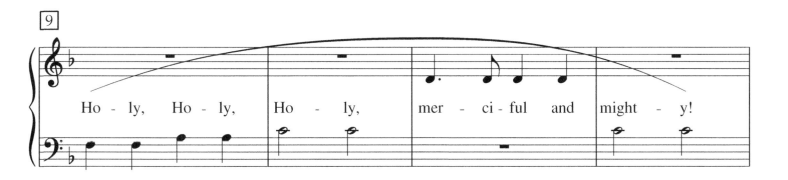

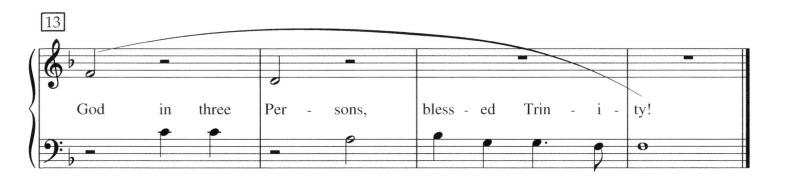

Student Position

One octave higher when performing as a duet

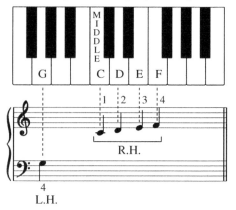

Hush, Little Baby
Optional Teacher Accompaniment

Carolina Folk Lullaby
Arranged by Glenda Austin

Hush, Little Baby

Carolina Folk Lullaby
Arranged by Glenda Austin

Play both hands one octave higher when performing as a duet.

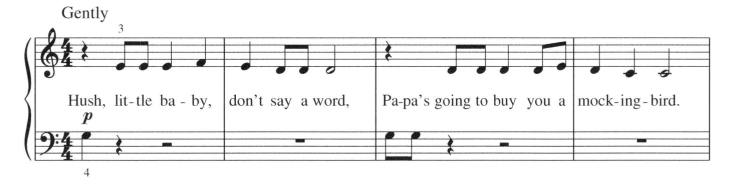

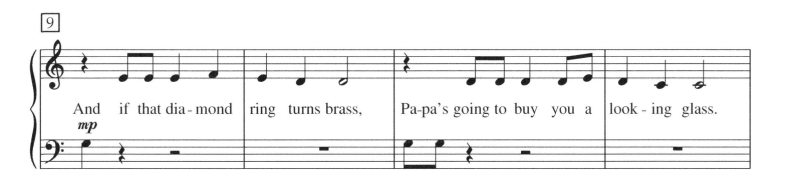

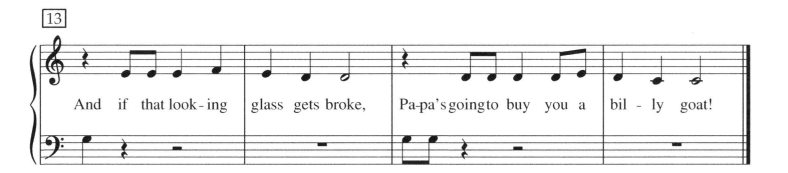

52

Original Yiddish (by Mikhl Gelbart):
Ich bin a kleyner dreydl,
Gemacht bin ich fun blay,
Kumt, lomir ale shpiln,
In dreydl eyns, tsvey, dray.
Oy, dreydl, dreydl, dreydl,
Oy, drey zich, dreydl, drey,
To, kumtzhe ale shpiln,
In dreydl eyns un tsvey.

Student Position
One octave higher when performing as a duet

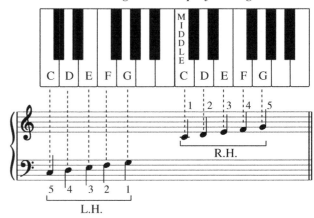

I Have a Little Dreydl
Optional Teacher Accompaniment

Words by S.S. Grossman
Music by S.E. Goldfarb
Arranged by Eric Baumgartner

I Have a Little Dreydl

Words by S.S. Grossman
Music by S.E. Goldfarb
Arranged by Eric Baumgartner

Play both hands one octave higher when performing as a duet.

Happily

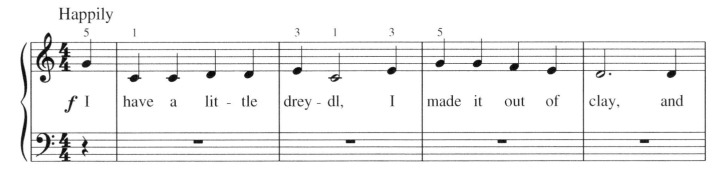

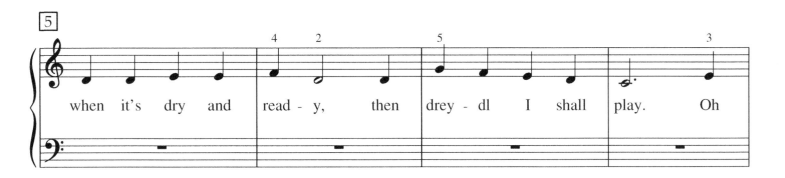

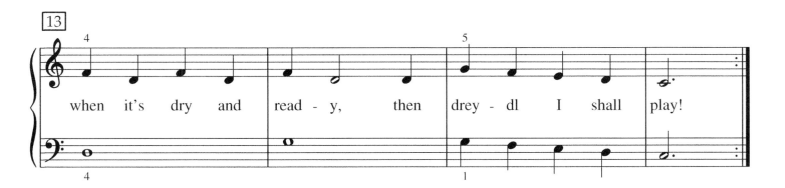

Watch Out!
Left hand gets to JUMP OVER the right hand in measure 9 for the High C!

Student Position
One octave higher when performing as a duet

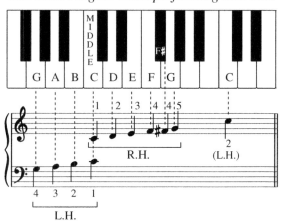

If You're Happy and You Know It
Optional Teacher Accompaniment

Words and Music by L. Smith
Arranged by Glenda Austin

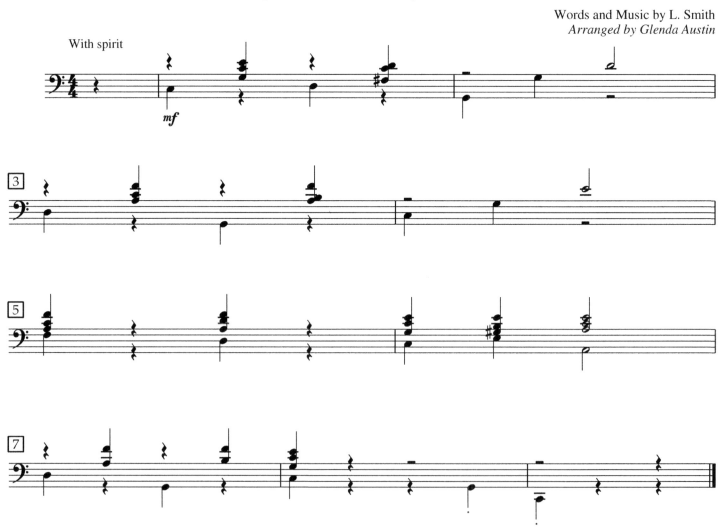

If You're Happy and You Know It

Words and Music by L. Smith
Arranged by Glenda Austin

Play both hands one octave higher when performing as a duet.

With spirit

If you're hap - py and you know it, clap your hands! *(clap, clap)* If you're

hap - py and you know it, clap your hands! *(clap, clap)* If you're

hap - py and you know it, then your face will sure - ly show it. If you're

hap - py and you know it, clap your hands!

L.H.

56

JASMINE FLOWER is a well-loved Chinese melody that in many ways symbolizes the beauty and grace of China. In fact, a recording of this song was recently launched into space as part of an American space capsule intended to introduce Earth's cultures to the (possible) residents of other planets!

Prepare!—
In measures 20-21, the L.H. crosses over the R.H. to play C. Keep the R.H. in the same position as you do this.

Student Position
One octave higher when performing as a duet

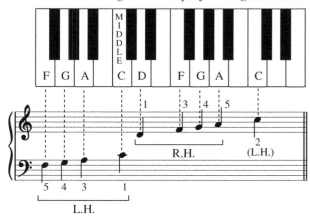

Jasmine Flower
Optional Teacher Accompaniment

Traditional Chinese Folk Song
Arranged by Carolyn C. Setliff

Jasmine Flower

Traditional Chinese Folk Song
Arranged by Carolyn C. Setliff

Play both hands one octave higher when performing as a duet.

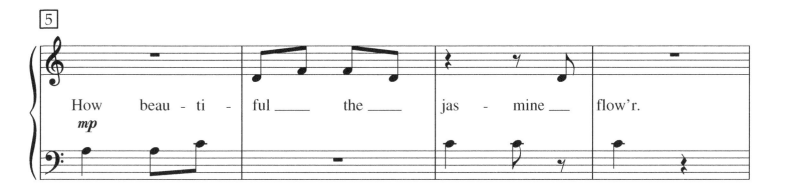

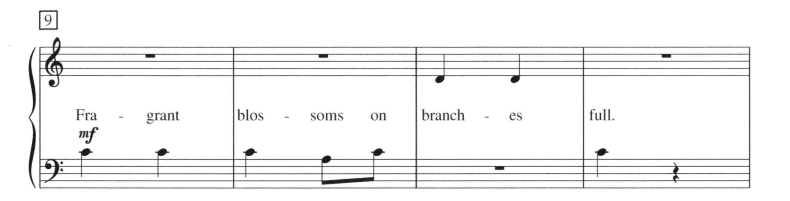

Optional Teacher Accompaniment

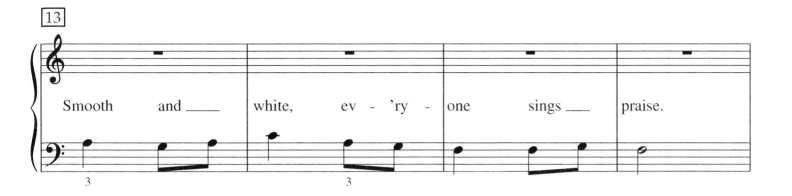

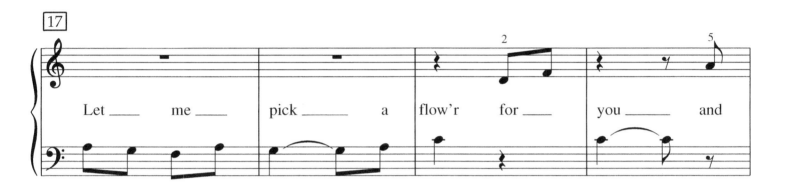

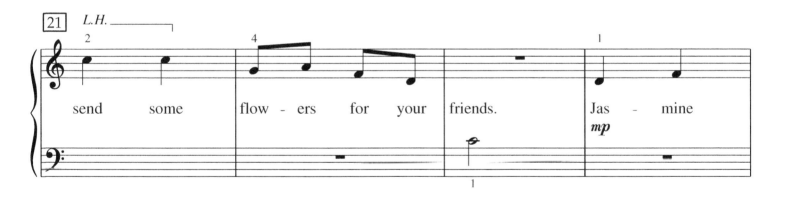

60

Hint!—
All the action in "Jingle Bells" takes place in the right hand. But the left hand does get the last word in, so be ready!

Student Position
One octave higher when performing as a duet

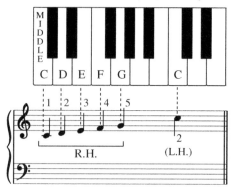

Jingle Bells
Optional Teacher Accompaniment

Words and Music by J. Pierpont
Arranged by Carolyn Miller

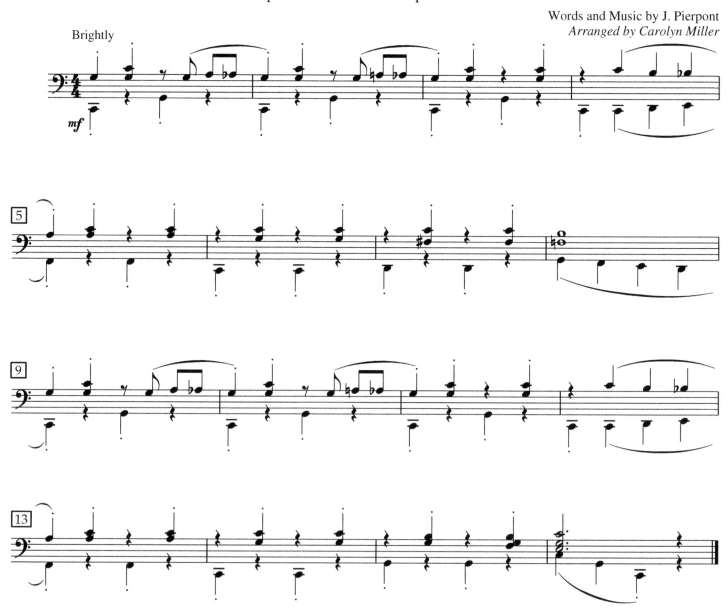

Jingle Bells

Words and Music by J. Pierpont
Arranged by Carolyn Miller

Play both hands one octave higher when performing as a duet.

Jin - gle bells! Jin - gle bells! Jin - gle all the way!

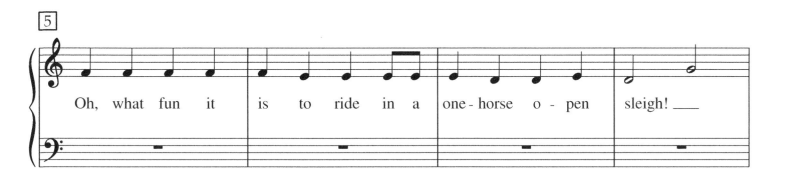

Oh, what fun it is to ride in a one - horse o - pen sleigh! ___

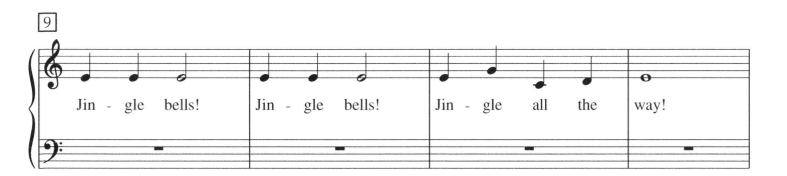

Jin - gle bells! Jin - gle bells! Jin - gle all the way!

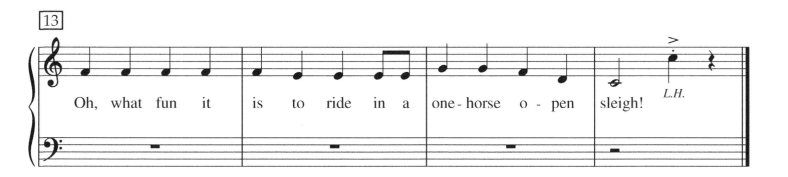

Oh, what fun it is to ride in a one - horse o - pen sleigh!

Student Position

One octave higher when performing as a duet

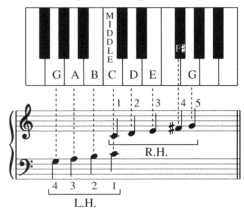

Joy to the World
Optional Teacher Accompaniment

Words by Isaac Watts
Music by George Frideric Handel
Adapted by Lowell Mason
Arranged by Carolyn Miller

Joy to the World

Words by Isaac Watts
Music by George Frideric Handel
Adapted by Lowell Mason
Arranged by Carolyn Miller

Play both hands one octave higher when performing as a duet.

Brightly

Joy to the world! the Lord is come; Let earth re - ceive her

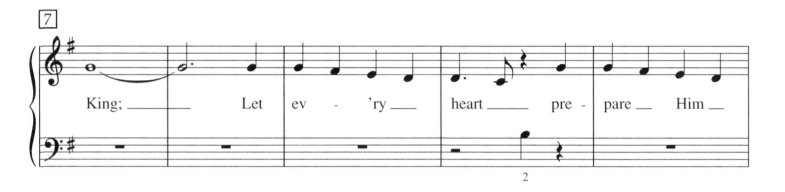

King; _____ Let ev - 'ry _____ heart _____ pre - pare _____ Him _____

room, _____ And heav'n and na - ture _ sing, And _ heav'n and na - ture _

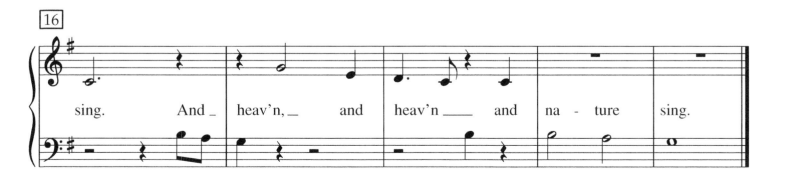

sing. And _ heav'n, _ and heav'n _____ and na - ture sing.

Student Position

One octave higher when performing as a duet

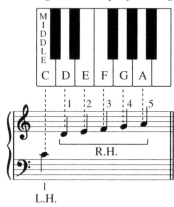

Kum Ba Yah

Optional Teacher Accompaniment

Traditional Spiritual
Arranged by Mary K. Sallee

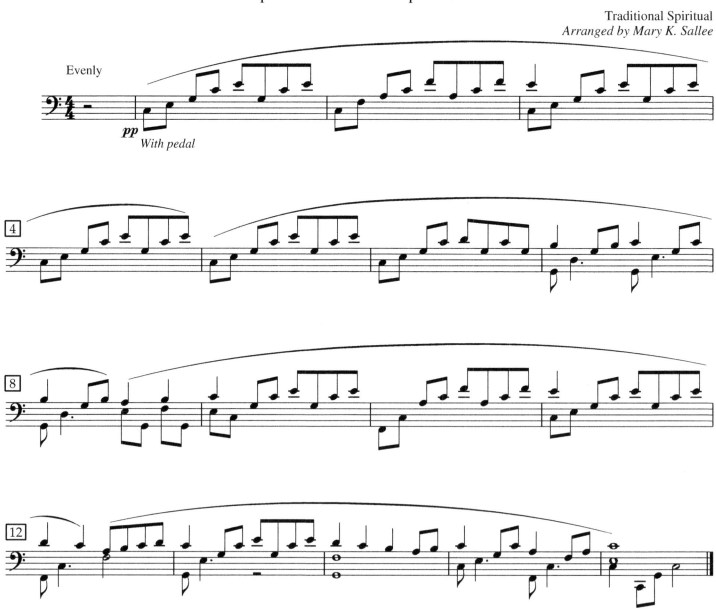

Kum Ba Yah

Traditional Spiritual
Arranged by Mary K. Sallee

Play both hands one octave higher when performing as a duet.

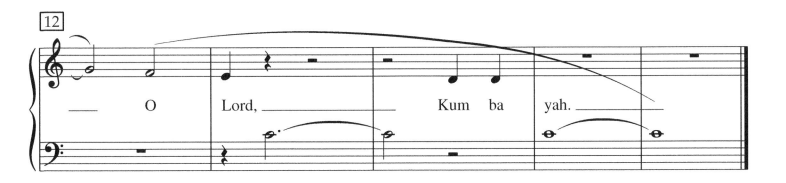

Student Position

One octave higher when performing as a duet

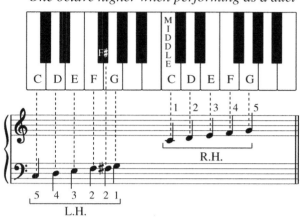

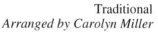

Lightly Row
Optional Teacher Accompaniment

Traditional
Arranged by Carolyn Miller

Happily

Lightly Row

Traditional
Arranged by Carolyn Miller

Play both hands one octave higher when performing as a duet.

Happily

Student Position
One octave higher when performing as a duet

Little Boogie
Optional Teacher Accompaniment

Carolyn Miller

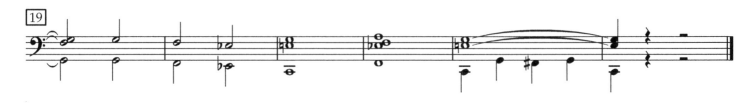

Little Boogie

Carolyn Miller

Play both hands one octave higher when performing as a duet.

Lively

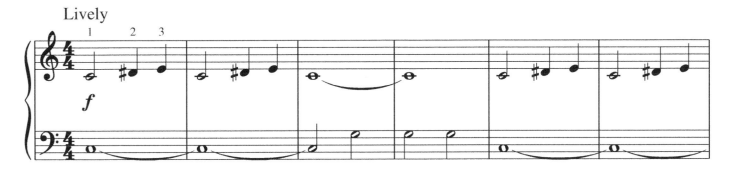

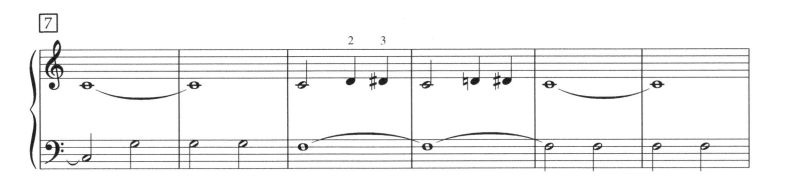

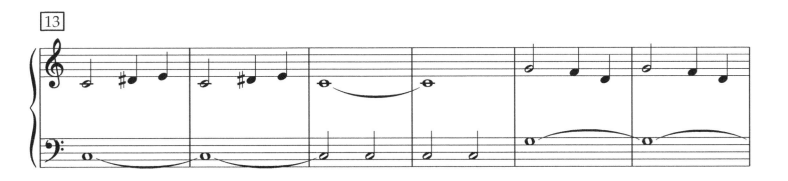

Did You Know?—

"A Little Night Music" *(Eine Kleine Nachtmusik* in German) is the main theme from Mozart's *Serenade No. 13 for Strings* (K.525), and is one of the most recognizable tunes in the history of music.

Student Position

One octave higher when performing as a duet

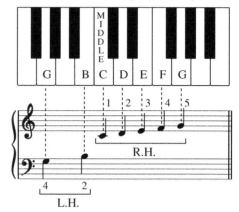

A Little Night Music

Optional Teacher Accompaniment

Wolfgang Amadeus Mozart (1756–91)
Arranged by Randall Hartsell

A Little Night Music

Wolfgang Amadeus Mozart (1756–91)
Arranged by Randall Hartsell

Play both hands one octave higher when performing as a duet.

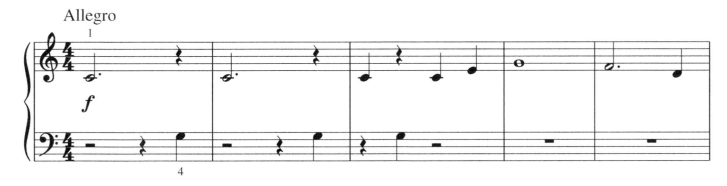

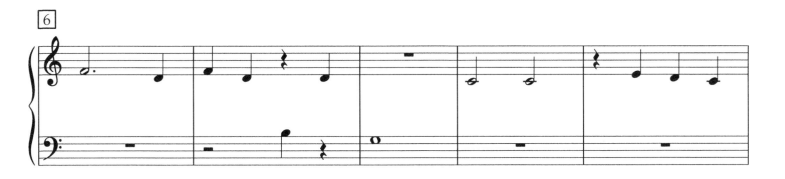

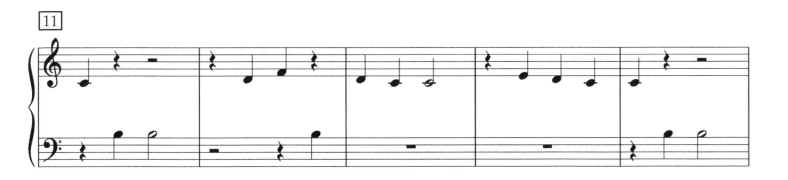

Little White Dove is another traditional
Spanish/Mexican melody so catchy and irresistible
that you MUST sing or hum while performing it!

Rhythm Hints—
1. The melody begins on beat 2.
2. Find all the tied notes and count these measures
   aloud, pointing to each note.

Student Position
One octave higher when performing as a duet

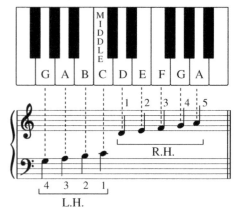

Little White Dove
Optional Teacher Accompaniment

Traditional
Arranged by Carolyn C. Setliff

In Waltz time

Little White Dove

Traditional
Arranged by Carolyn C. Setliff

Play both hands one octave higher when performing as a duet.

In Waltz time

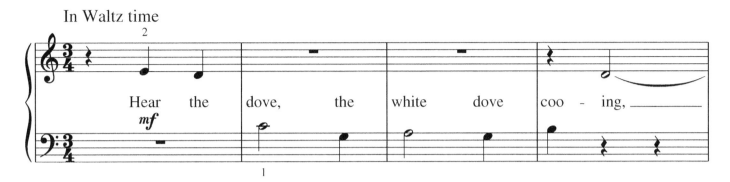

Hear the dove, the white dove coo - ing, _____

mf

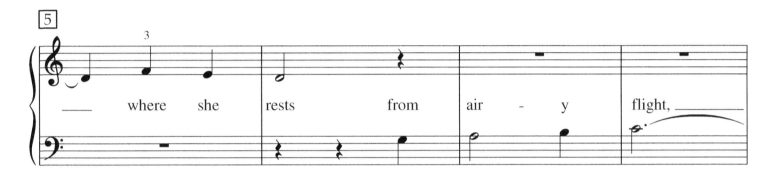

5

___ where she rests from air - y flight, _____

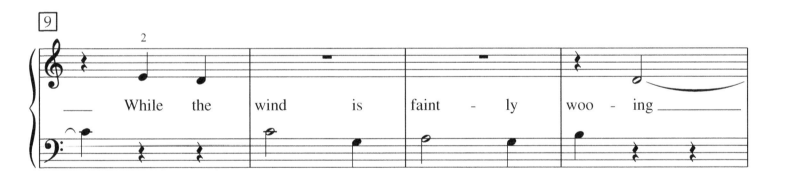

9

___ While the wind is faint - ly woo - ing _____

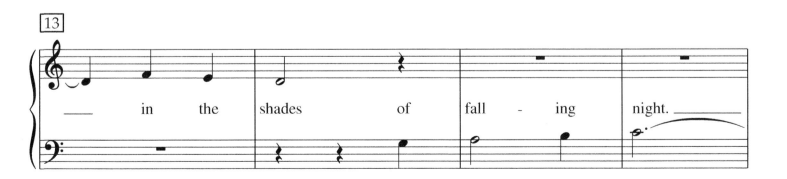

13

___ in the shades of fall - ing night. _____

74

Optional Teacher Accompaniment

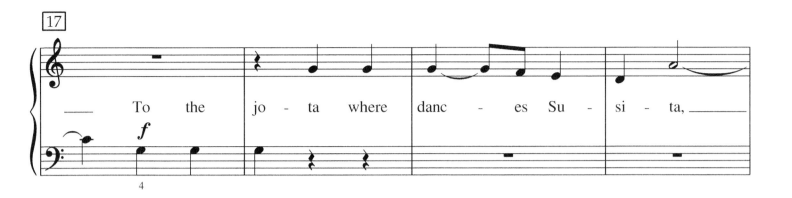

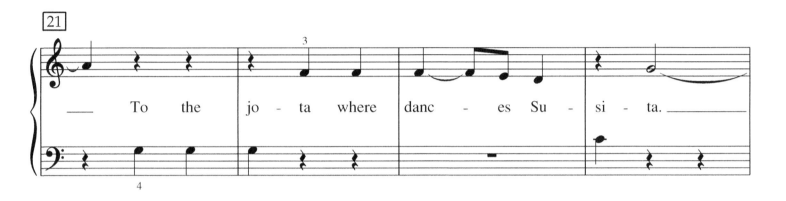

76

Student Position

One octave higher when performing as a duet

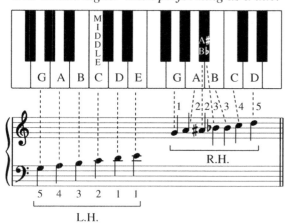

Intervals

An *interval* is the distance between two notes. The L.H. plays three different *intervals* in this piece. G to D is a 5th, G to E is a 6th and C to E is a 3rd. Practice each separately so that you become an expert at switching between them quickly!

Two Names for the Same Black Key— A♯ and B♭ are the same black key. They are called *enharmonics.*

Lonely and Blue
Optional Teacher Accompaniment

Carolyn Miller

Slowly

Lonely and Blue

Carolyn Miller

Play as written when performing as a duet.

Slowly *

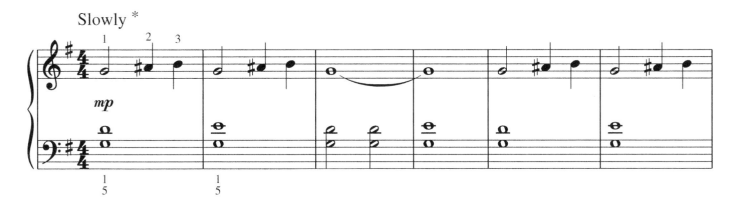

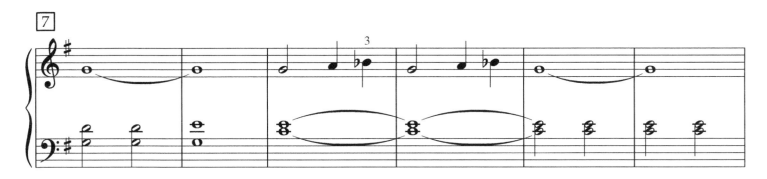

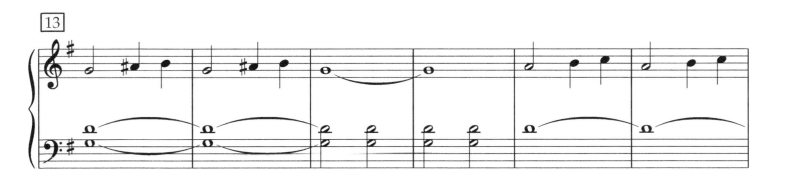

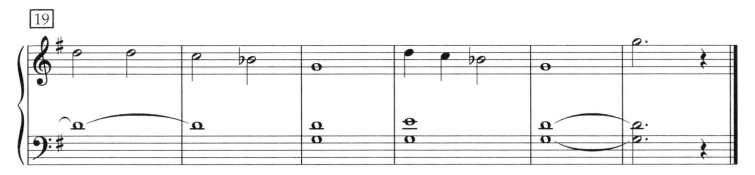

* For fun, try playing this piece as quickly as you can!

Did You Know?—
In addition to major works for orchestra and solo piano, Brahms wrote over 200 beautiful songs. This famous lullaby was written to celebrate the birth of a friend's son.

Student Position

One octave higher when performing as a duet

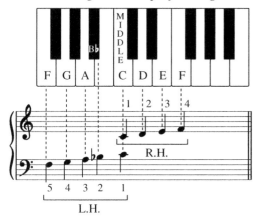

Lullaby

Optional Teacher Accompaniment

Johannes Brahms (1833–97)
Arranged by Randall Hartsell

Lullaby

Johannes Brahms (1833–97)
Arranged by Randall Hartsell

Play both hands one octave higher when performing as a duet.

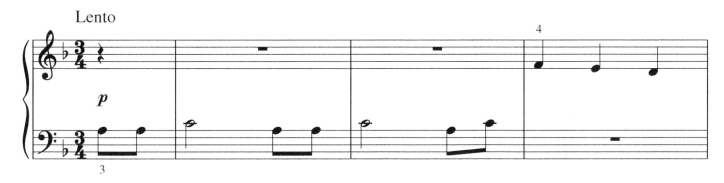

Did You Know?—
It is not exactly clear who wrote the words and music to "The Marine's Hymn." An unknown Marine is said to have written the words in 1847 (currently attributed to Henry C. Davis). The music may have come from the French composer, Jacques Offenbach. Offenbach used this wonderful melody in his 1867 comic opera, *Genéviève de Brabant*. Some believe, however, that the tune actually comes from a Spanish folk song, written well before Offenbach's opera.

Student Position
One octave higher when performing as a duet

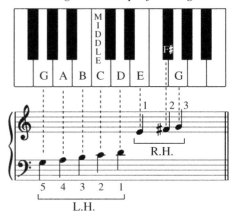

The Marine's Hymn
Optional Teacher Accompaniment

Words by Henry C. Davis
Melody based on a theme by Jacques Offenbach
Arranged by Eric Baumgartner

The Marine's Hymn

Words by Henry C. Davis
Melody based on a theme by Jacques Offenbach
Arranged by Eric Baumgartner

Play both hands one octave higher when performing as a duet.

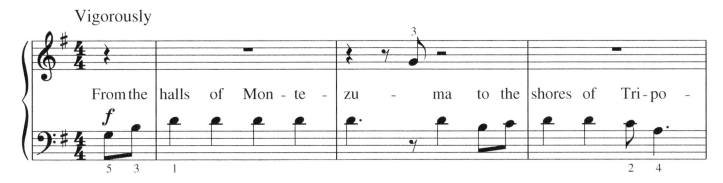

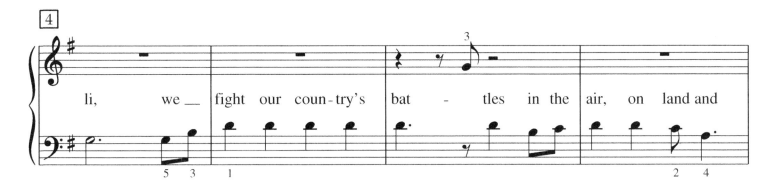

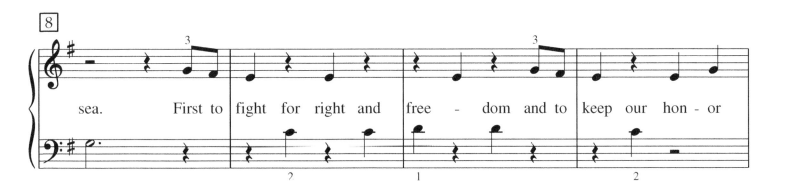

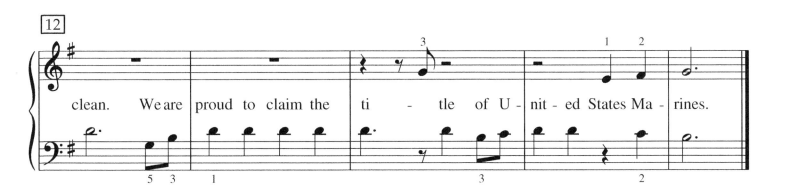

The ELVIS Connection—
" 'O Sole Mio" is one of Italy's best-known love songs, invoking to many the beauty and romanticism of Italian culture. Elvis Presley liked the tune so much he used its melody to record a song called "It's Now or Never," which went straight to #1 in 1960.

Reminder—
The first beat is a rest!

Student Position
One octave higher when performing as a duet

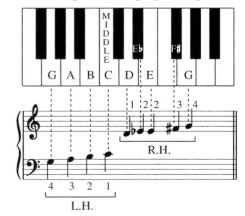

'O Sole Mio
Optional Teacher Accompaniment

Words by Giovanni Capurro
Music by Eduardo di Capua (1865–1917)
Arranged by Carolyn C. Setliff

Andantino

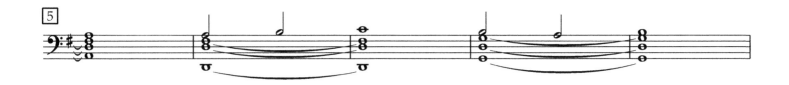

'O Sole Mio
(My Own Sun)

Words by Giovanni Capurro
Music by Eduardo di Capua (1865–1917)
Arranged by Carolyn C. Setliff

Play both hands one octave higher when performing as a duet.

Andantino

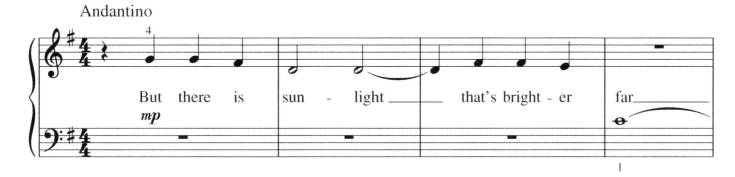

But there is sun - light _____ that's bright - er far_____

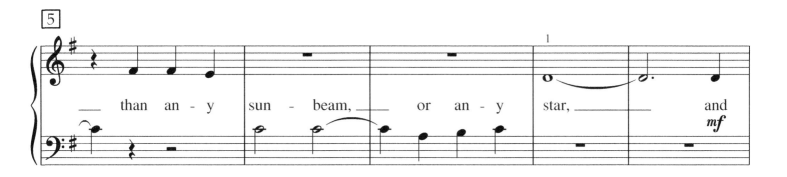

_____ than an - y sun - beam, _____ or an - y star, _____ and

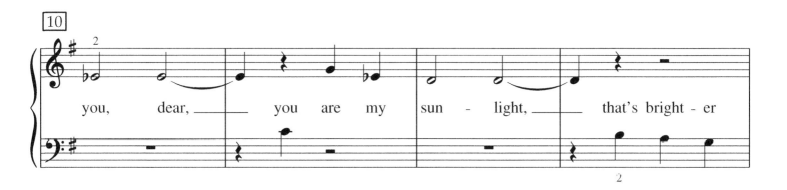

you, dear, _____ you are my sun - light, _____ that's bright - er

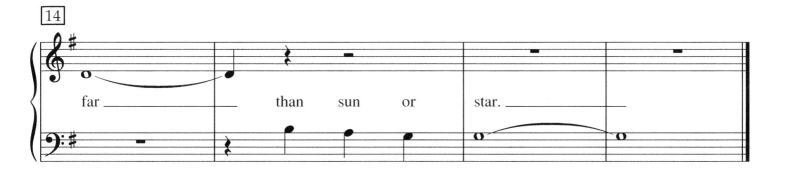

far _____ _____ than sun or star. _____

84

Student Position
One octave higher when performing as a duet

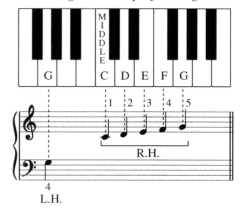

Ode to Joy
Optional Teacher Accompaniment

Ludwig van Beethoven (1770–1827)
Arranged by Randall Hartsell

Ode to Joy

Ludwig van Beethoven (1770–1827)
Arranged by Randall Hartsell

Play both hands one octave higher when performing as a duet.

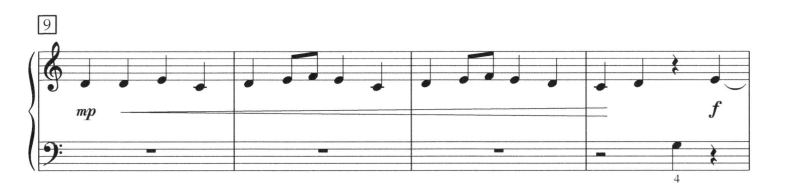

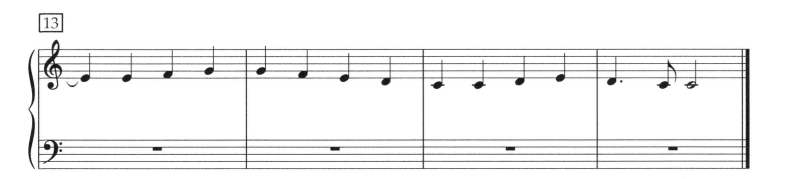

Student Position

One octave higher when performing as a duet

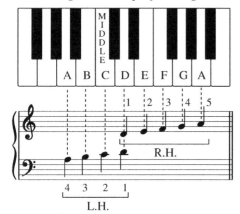

Oh Hanukkah is perhaps the most celebrated Hanukkah song, and is also danceable as a hora.

Original Yiddish (by Mordkhe Rivesman):
Oy Chanuke, oy Chanuke, a yontif, a sheyner, a
 Lustiker, a freylecher, nito noch azeyner.
Alle nacht in dreydlech shpiln mir,
Zudik-heyse latkes est on a shier.
Geshvinder tsindt kinder.
Di dininke lichtelach on.
Zogt 'Al hanissim,' loybt Gott far di nisim,
Un kumt gicher tantsn in kon.

Oh Hanukkah
Optional Teacher Accompaniment

Chassidic Melody
Arranged by Eric Baumgartner

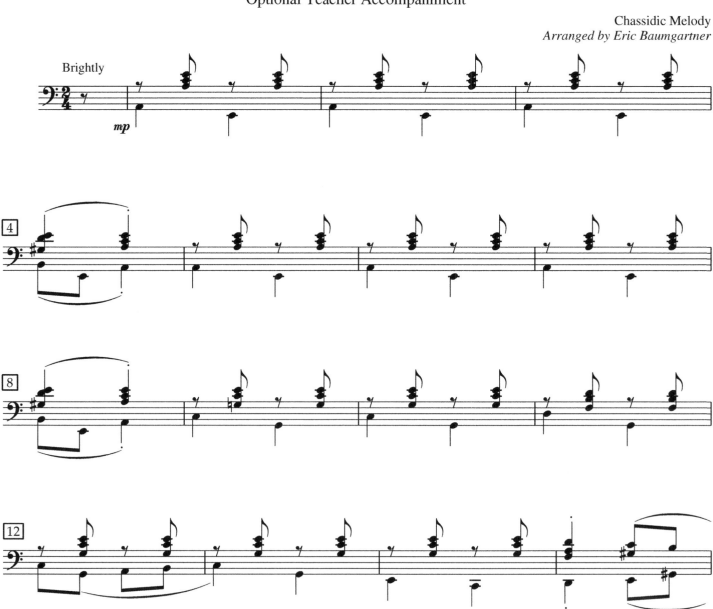

Oh Hanukkah

Chassidic Melody
Arranged by Eric Baumgartner

Play both hands one octave higher when performing as a duet.

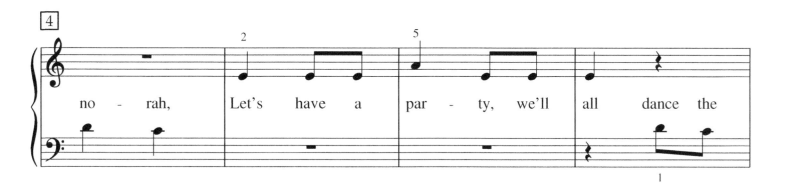

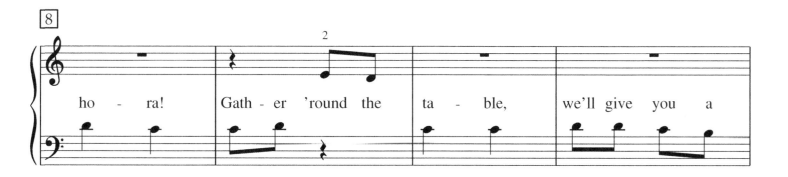

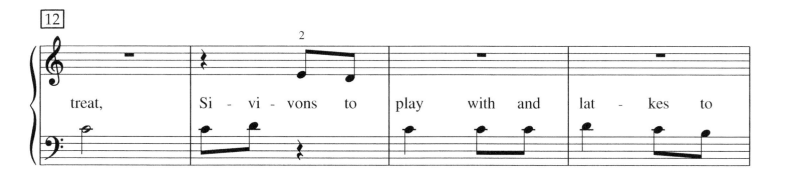

Optional Teacher Accompaniment

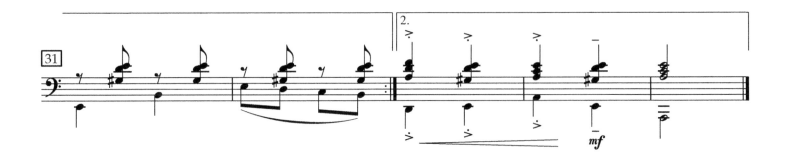

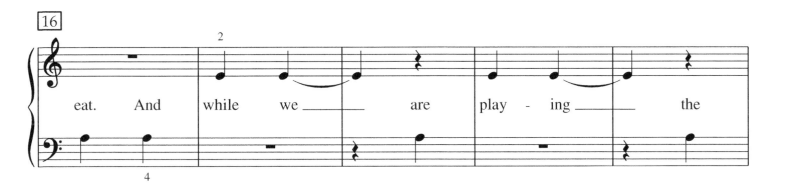

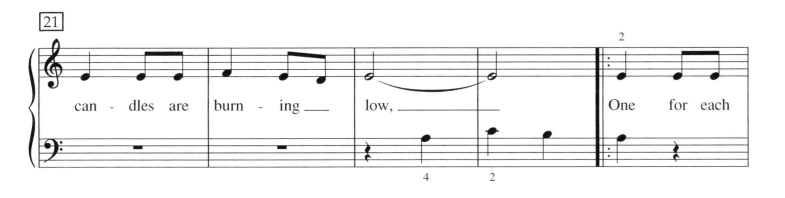

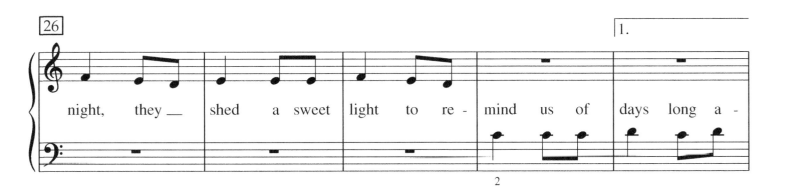

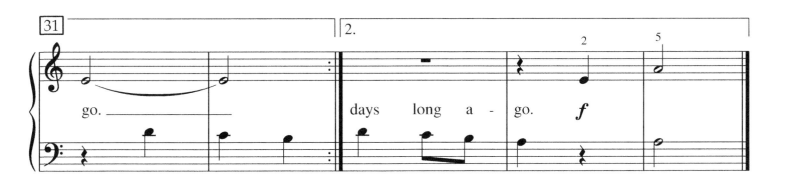

Student Position
One octave higher when performing as a duet

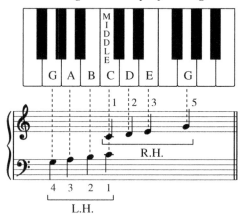

On Top of Old Smoky
Optional Teacher Accompaniment

Kentucky Mountain Folk Song
Arranged by Glenda Austin

On Top of Old Smoky

Kentucky Mountain Folk Song
Arranged by Glenda Austin

Play both hands one octave higher when performing as a duet.

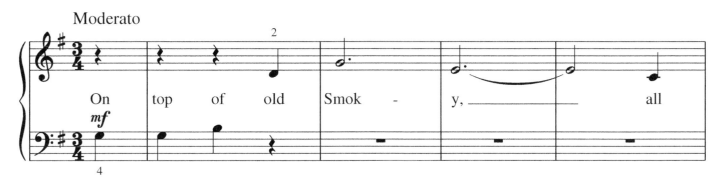

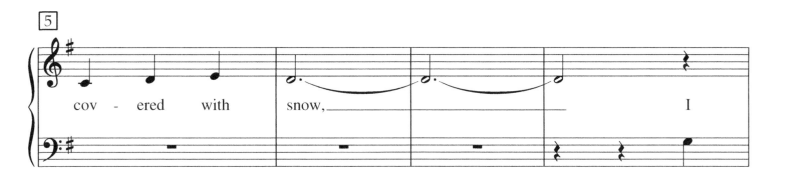

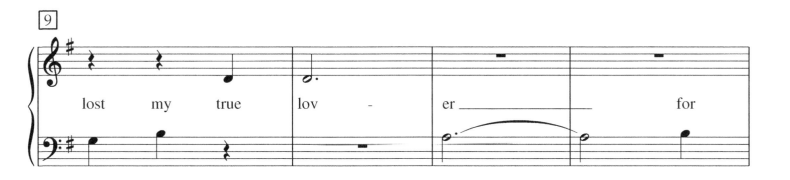

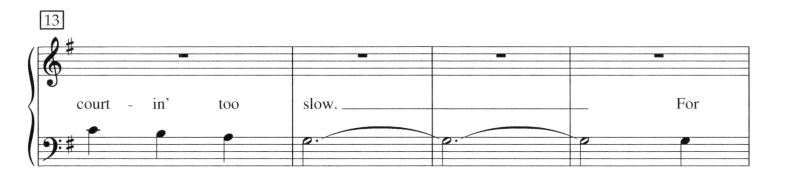

Optional Teacher Accompaniment

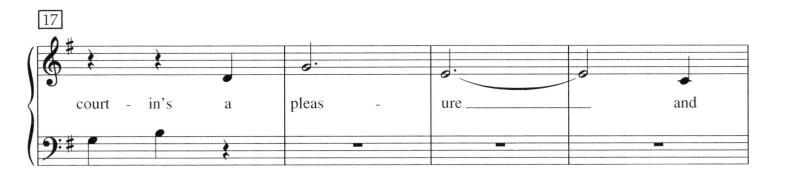

court - in's a pleas - ure _____ and

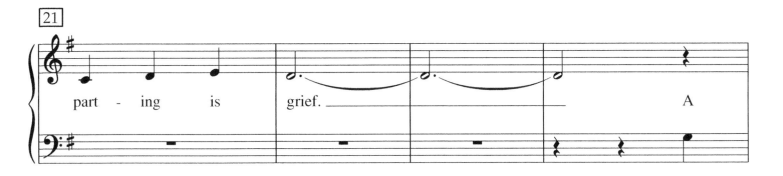

part - ing is grief. _____ A

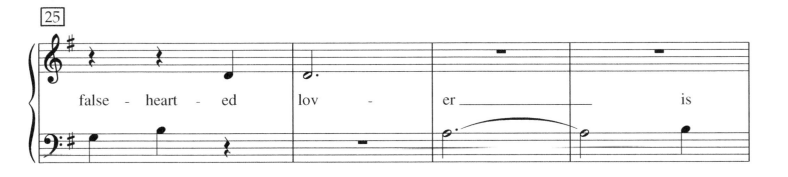

false - heart - ed lov - er _____ is

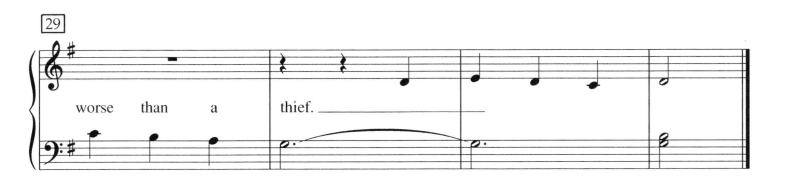

worse than a thief. _____

Student Position

One octave higher when performing as a duet

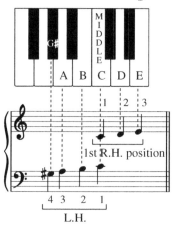

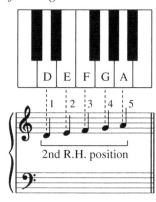

Peaceful Waters
Optional Teacher Accompaniment

Eric Baumgartner

Peaceful Waters

Eric Baumgartner

Play both hands one octave higher when performing as a duet.

Gently

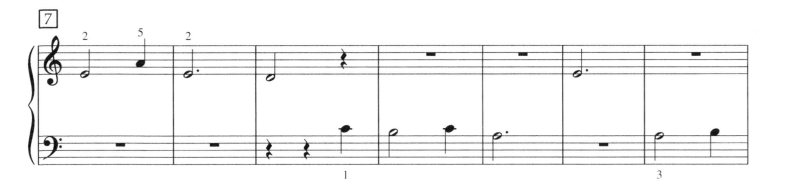

gradually get softer and slower

Pitter-Patter

Carolyn Miller

Play as written when performing as a duet.

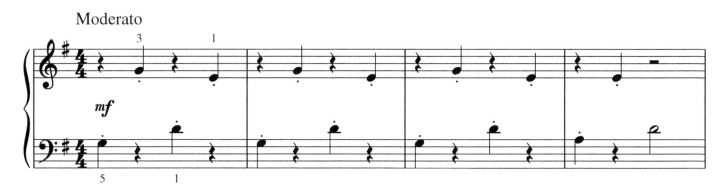

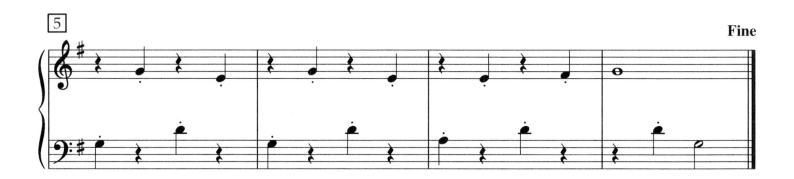

REMINDERS:

D.C. al Fine–
Go back to the beginning and play to the
Fine (end).

- Do you remember what *staccato* means?

  drip, drop

- There are only two F♯'s in "Pitter-Patter."
  Can you find them?

Student Position

Play as written when performing as a duet

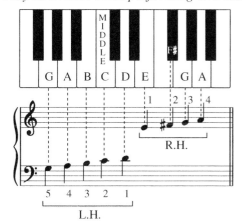

Pitter-Patter
Optional Teacher Accompaniment

Carolyn Miller

Student Position

One octave higher when performing as a duet

Ready, Set, Rock!
Optional Teacher Accompaniment

Eric Baumgartner

With energy

Ready, Set, Rock!

Eric Baumgartner

Play both hands one octave higher when performing as a duet.

With energy

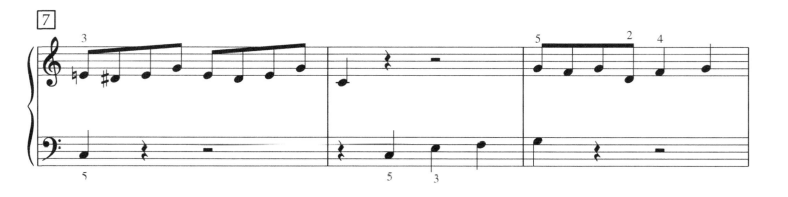

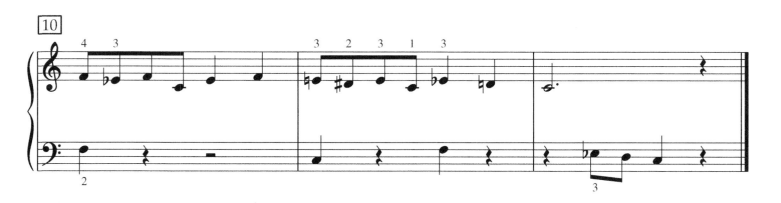

Student Position
Play as written when performing as a duet

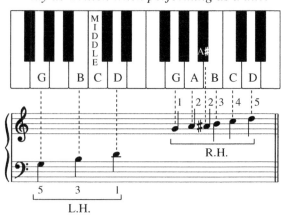

Rock-a-My Soul
Optional Teacher Accompaniment

African-American Spiritual
Arranged by Carolyn Miller

Spirited

mf

5

9

14

1.

2.

Rock-a-My Soul

African-American Spiritual
Arranged by Carolyn Miller

Play as written when performing as a duet.

Spirited

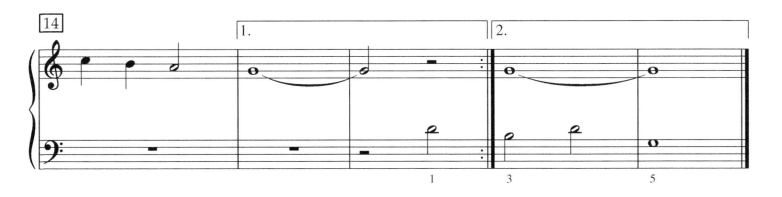

Did You Know?—
Legend has it that the beautiful words to
"Silent Night" (*Stille Nacht* in German) were
written in much haste, minutes before midnight
Mass was to begin, because some mischievous
mice had nibbled through the bellows of the
mighty organ. As a result, this Christmas classic
was sung quietly with soft guitar, and somehow
captured the perfect mood and sentiment for the
season. It remains a favorite throughout the
world.

Student Position
One octave higher when performing as a duet

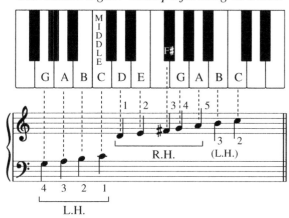

Silent Night
Optional Teacher Accompaniment

Words by Joseph Mohr
Translated by John F. Young
Music by Franz X. Gruber
Arranged by Carolyn Miller

Silent Night

Words by Joseph Mohr
Translated by John F. Young
Music by Franz X. Gruber
Arranged by Carolyn Miller

Play both hands one octave higher when performing as a duet.

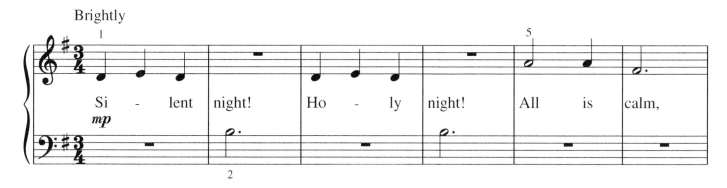

Si - lent night! Ho - ly night! All is calm,

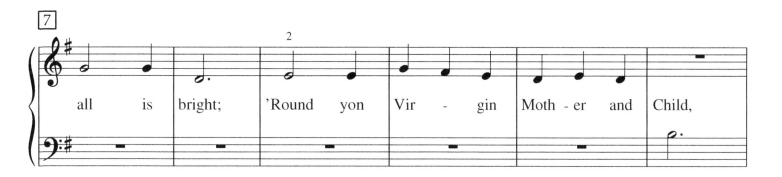

all is bright; 'Round yon Vir - gin Moth - er and Child,

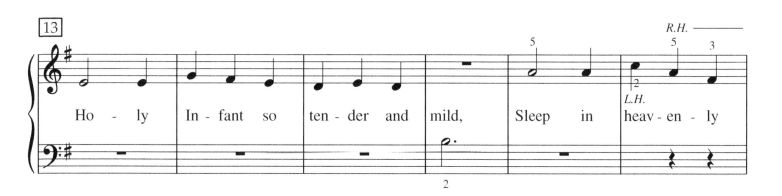

Ho - ly In - fant so ten - der and mild, Sleep in heav - en - ly

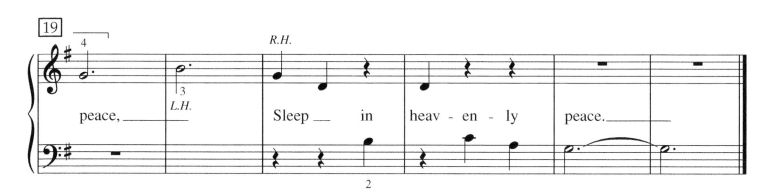

peace, ___ Sleep ___ in heav - en - ly peace. ___

> **Be prepared!** This piece changes hand positions several times.

Did You Know?—
The words to our national anthem were written by Francis Scott Key in 1814. He wrote them after witnessing a battle between the U.S. and England at Fort McHenry during the War of 1812. The morning after the long battle he was relieved to see "that our flag was still there" flying over the fort. The melody was well known before Key wrote his poem: it is from an English song, "Anacreon in Heaven."

The Star-Spangled Banner
Optional Teacher Accompaniment

Words by Francis Scott Key
Music by John Stafford Smith
Arranged by Eric Baumgartner

The Star-Spangled Banner

Words by Francis Scott Key
Music by John Stafford Smith
Arranged by Eric Baumgartner

Play both hands one octave higher when performing as a duet.

Proudly

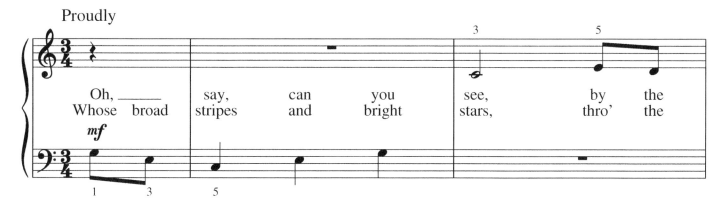

Oh, _____ say, can you see, by the
Whose broad stripes and bright stars, thro' the

mf

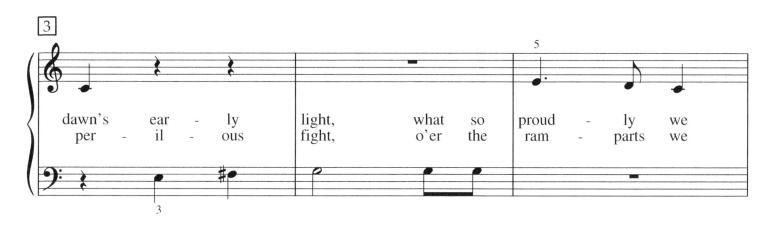

dawn's ear - ly light, what so proud - ly we
per - il - ous fight, o'er the ram - parts we

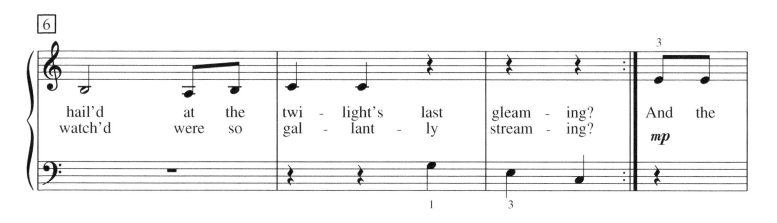

hail'd at the twi - light's last gleam - ing? And the
watch'd were so gal - lant - ly stream - ing?

mp

Optional Teacher Accompaniment

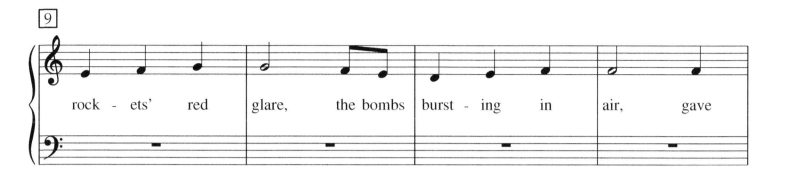

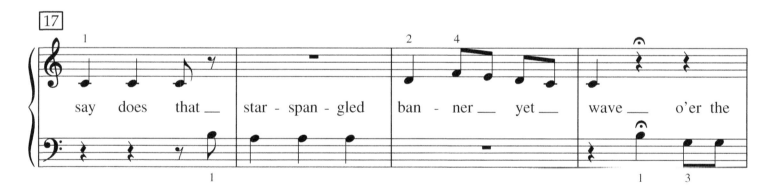

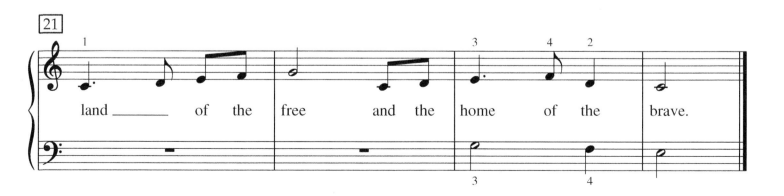

> **Remember**—all F's are sharped.
> Can you find eight F♯'s?

Student Position
One octave higher when performing as a duet

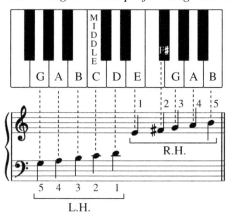

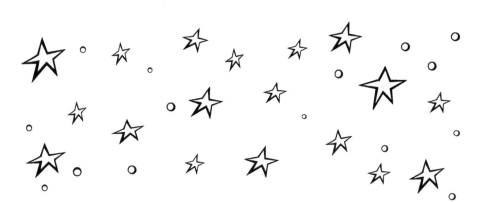

Stars
Optional Teacher Accompaniment

Carolyn Miller

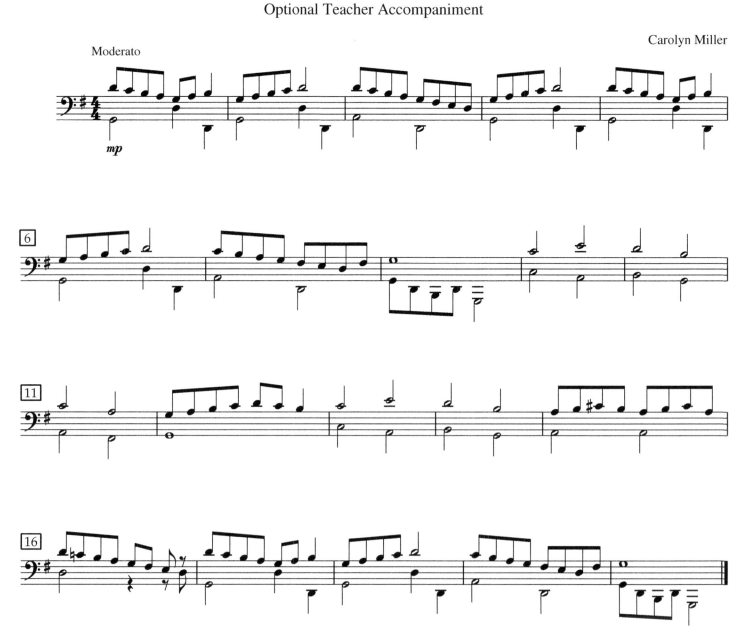

Moderato

mp

Stars

Carolyn Miller

Play both hands one octave higher when performing as a duet.

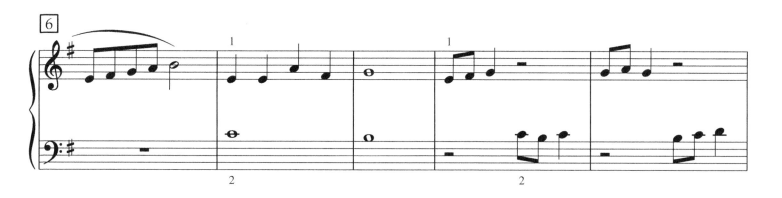

REMINDER:
Staccato—When a note has a dot under or over it, play the key like it's "hot"! The Italian word for this is *staccato* and it means to play crisply and detached.

Did You Know?—
Haydn is considered the "father of the symphony," and wrote over 100 of them. The "Surprise" Symphony is Symphony No. 94 in G Major, which he composed in 1791. (Ask your teacher why it's nicknamed the "Surprise" Symphony.)

Student Position
One octave higher when performing as a duet

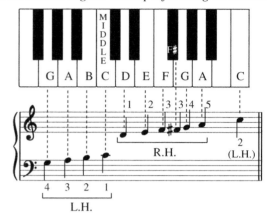

"Surprise" Symphony
Optional Teacher Accompaniment

Franz Joseph Haydn (1732–1809)
Arranged by Randall Hartsell

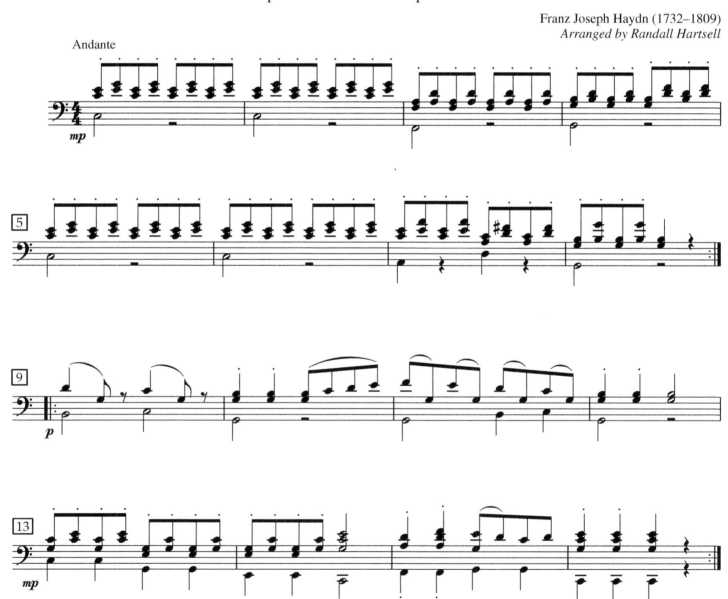

"Surprise" Symphony

Franz Joseph Haydn (1732–1809)
Arranged by Randall Hartsell

Play both hands one octave higher when performing as a duet.

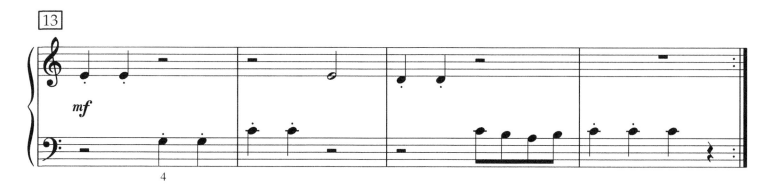

Did You Know?—
This is the best-loved song about America's pastime.
Even though it was written in 1908, it is still sung
at baseball games during the seventh inning stretch.
Jack Norworth wrote the lyrics first and then approached
Albert von Tilzer to compose the music. Oddly enough,
neither gentleman had ever attended a major league game
before writing this baseball classic!

Take Me Out to the Ball Game
Optional Teacher Accompaniment

Words by Jack Norworth
Music by Albert von Tilzer
Arranged by Eric Baumgartner

Take Me Out to the Ball Game

Words by Jack Norworth
Music by Albert von Tilzer
Arranged by Eric Baumgartner

Play both hands one octave higher when performing as a duet.

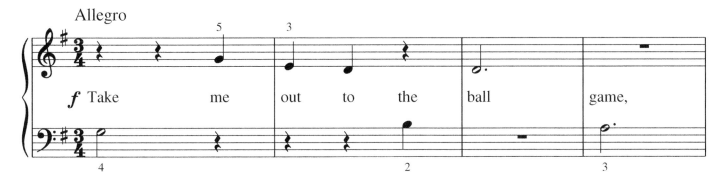

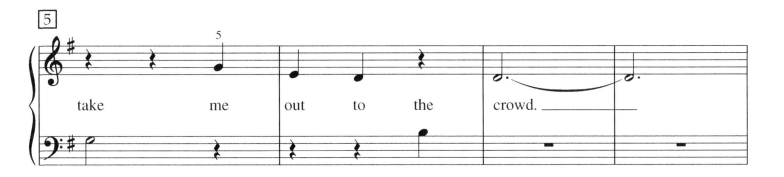

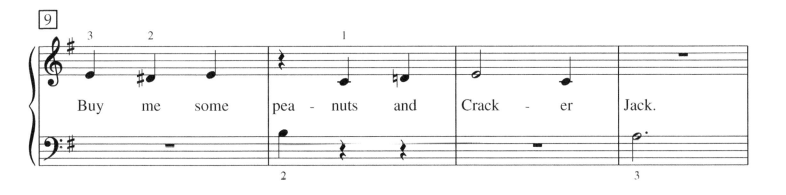

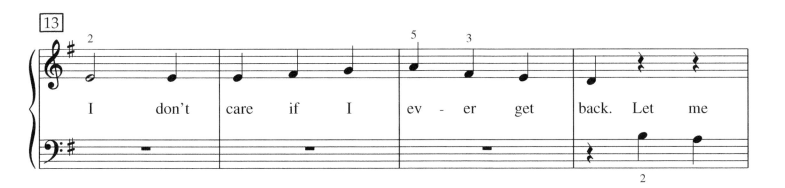

Optional Teacher Accompaniment

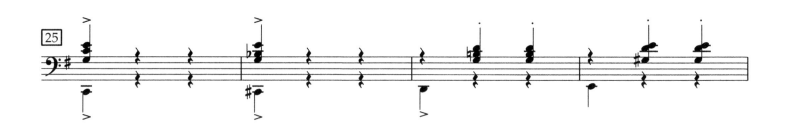

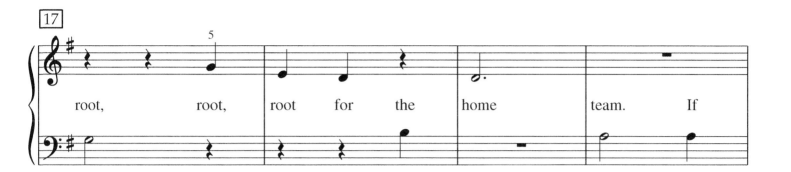

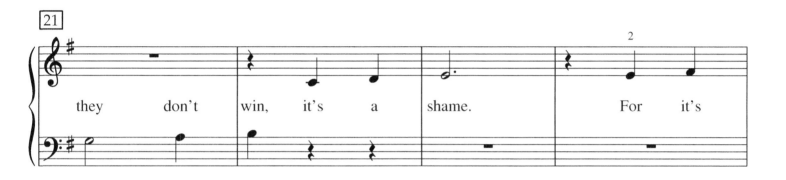

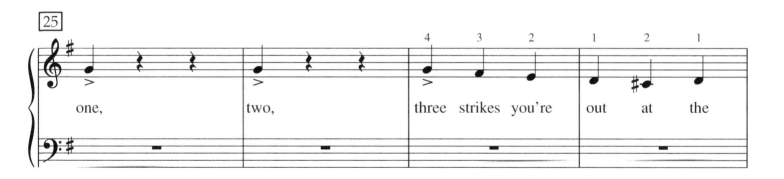

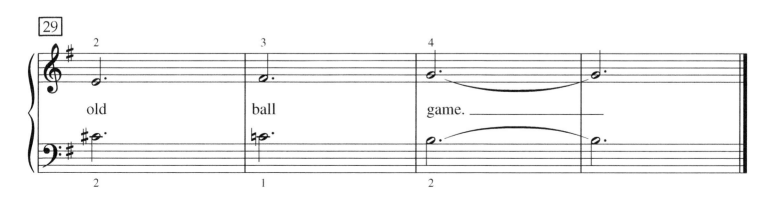

116

Hint!—
The R.H. five finger position is
a little different than usual, so
pay careful attention.

Student Position
One octave higher when performing as a duet

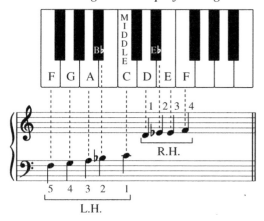

This 'n' That
Optional Teacher Accompaniment

Eric Baumgartner

With a steady Rock beat

This 'n' That

Eric Baumgartner

Play both hands one octave higher when performing as a duet.

With a steady Rock beat

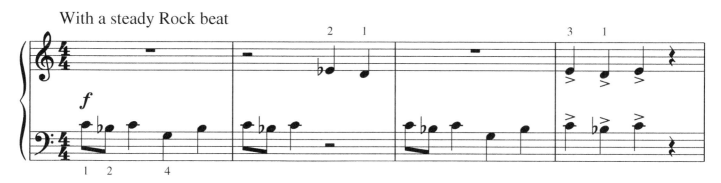

Cross-Overs

*2 over 1,
And it's fun!
Left hand gets to do it first–
Right hand gets to try it later!*

Student Position
Play as written when performing as a duet

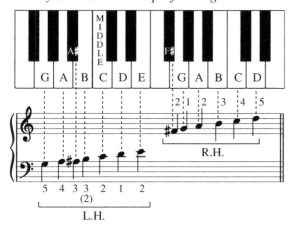

This Old Man
Optional Teacher Accompaniment

Traditional
Arranged by Carolyn Miller

Happily

This Old Man

Traditional
Arranged by Carolyn Miller

Play as written when performing as a duet.

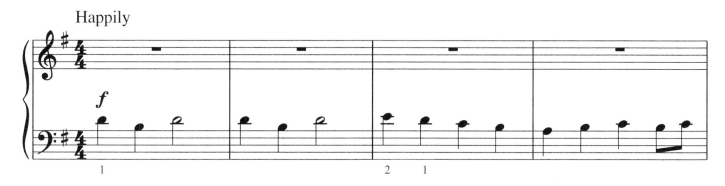

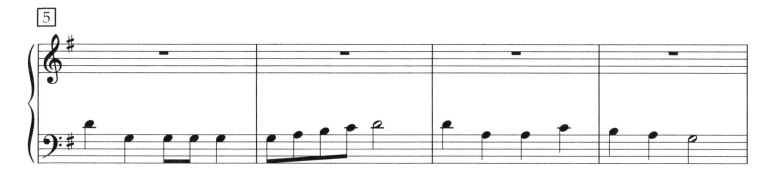

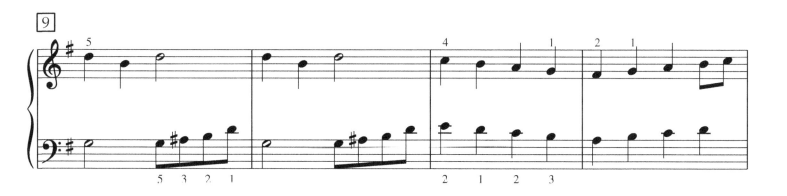

Traffic Jam

Eric Baumgartner

Play as written when performing as a duet.

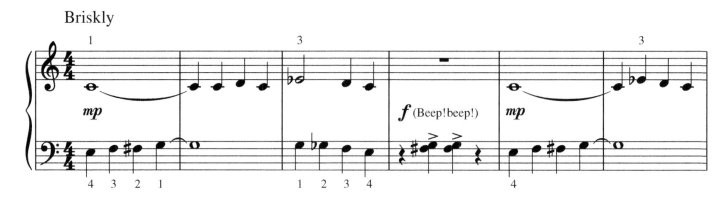

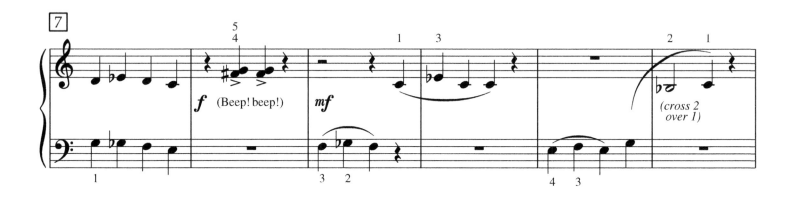

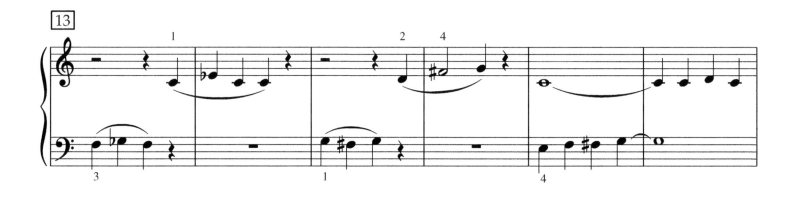

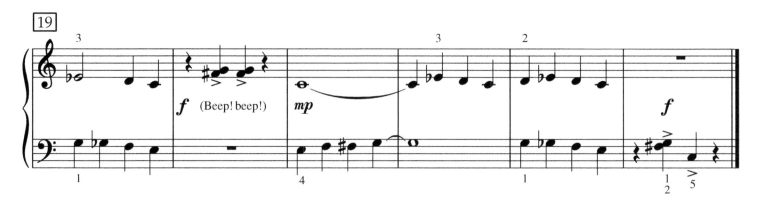

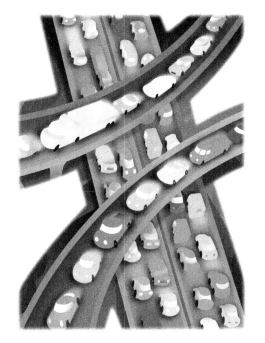

Student Position

Play as written when performing as a duet

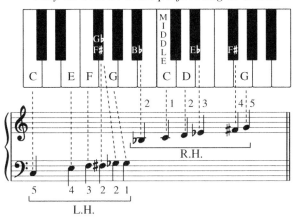

Traffic Jam
Optional Teacher Accompaniment

Eric Baumgartner

Briskly

122

Student Position
One octave higher when performing as a duet

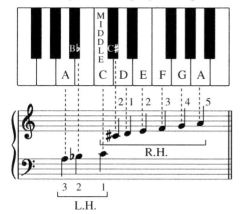

Turkish March
from *The Ruins of Athens*

Optional Teacher Accompaniment

Ludwig van Beethoven (1770–1827)
Arranged by Randall Hartsell

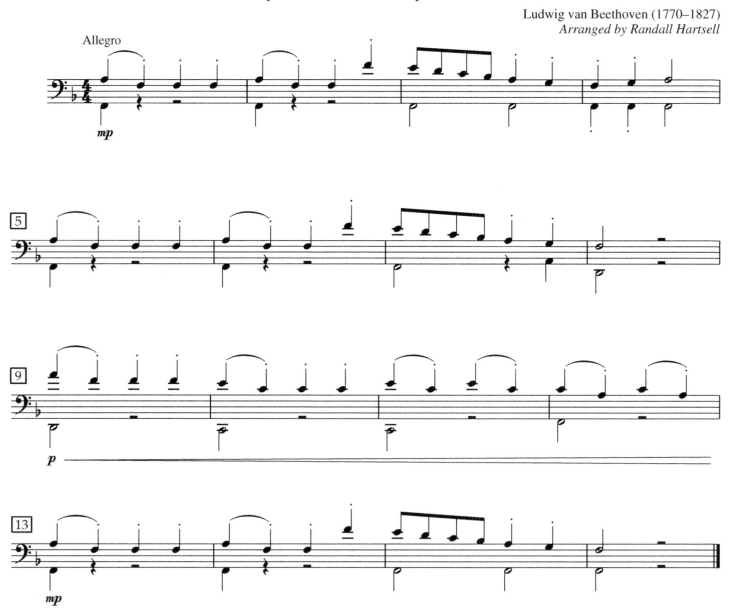

Turkish March
from *The Ruins of Athens*

Ludwig van Beethoven (1770–1827)
Arranged by Randall Hartsell

Play both hands one octave higher when performing as a duet.

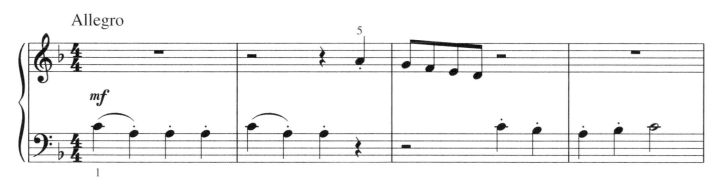

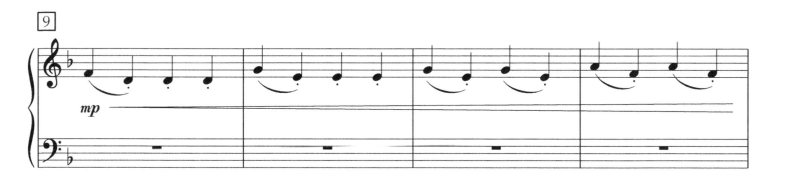

124

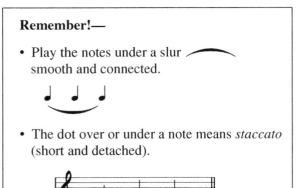

Remember!—

- Play the notes under a slur smooth and connected.

- The dot over or under a note means *staccato* (short and detached).

Student Position

One octave higher when performing as a duet

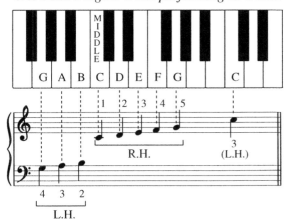

Wooden Shoe Waltz

Optional Teacher Accompaniment

Carolyn Miller

Wooden Shoe Waltz

Carolyn Miller

Play both hands one octave higher when performing as a duet.

With energy

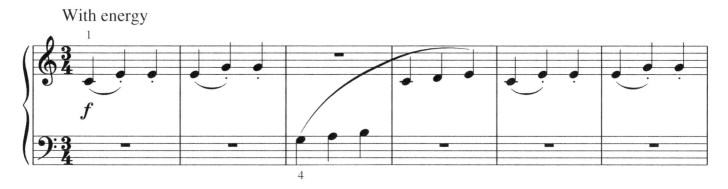

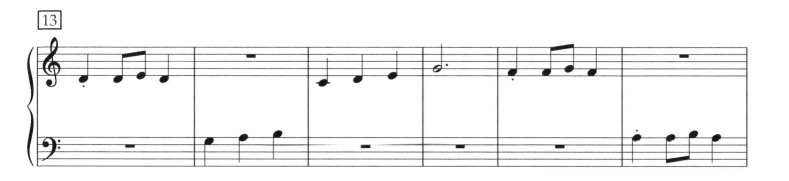

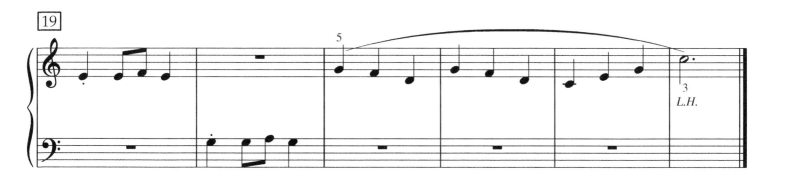

126

Did You Know?—
This is, perhaps, the most famous American folk song. It was very popular even before the Revolutionary War. Folk songs are often created by singing new words over older, familiar melodies. For example, the words to "Yankee Doodle," written by an unknown English army physician, are about our early American soldiers and are set to a melody that was already well known in England and in America.

Student Position
One octave higher when performing as a duet

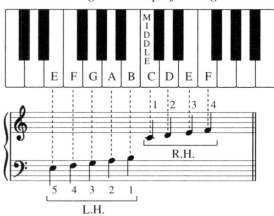

Yankee Doodle
Optional Teacher Accompaniment

Traditional
Arranged by Eric Baumgartner

Brightly

Yankee Doodle

Traditional
Arranged by Eric Baumgartner

Play both hands one octave higher when performing as a duet.

Brightly

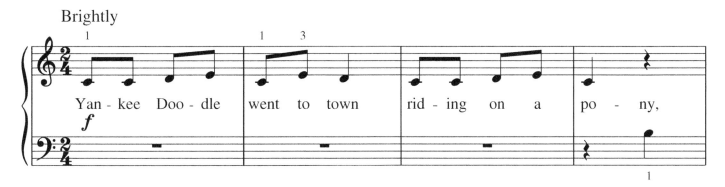

Yan - kee Doo - dle went to town rid - ing on a po - ny,

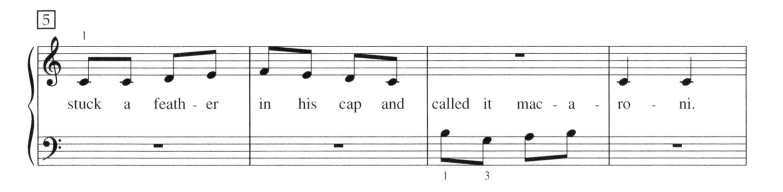

stuck a feath - er in his cap and called it mac - a - ro - ni.

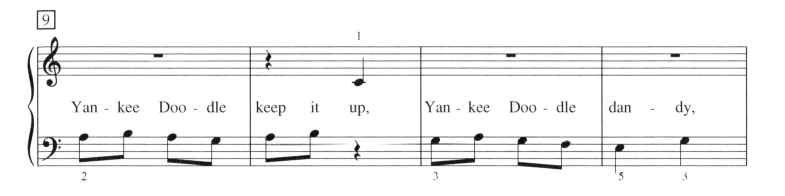

Yan - kee Doo - dle keep it up, Yan - kee Doo - dle dan - dy,

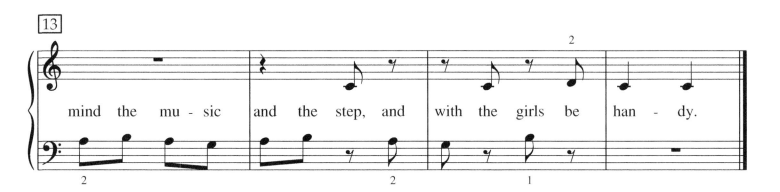

mind the mu - sic and the step, and with the girls be han - dy.

TEACHING LITTLE FINGERS TO PLAY MORE

TEACHING LITTLE FINGERS TO PLAY MORE
by Leigh Kaplan
Teaching Little Fingers to Play More is a fun-filled and colorfully illustrated follow-up book to *Teaching Little Fingers to Play*. It strengthens skills learned while carefully easing the transition into John Thompson's *Modern Course, First Grade*.
00406137 Book only $6.99
00406527 Book/Audio $9.99

SUPPLEMENTARY SERIES
All books include optional teacher accompaniments.

BROADWAY SONGS
arr. Carolyn Miller
MID TO LATER ELEMENTARY LEVEL
10 great show tunes for students to enjoy, including: Edelweiss • I Whistle a Happy Tune • I Won't Grow Up • Maybe • The Music of the Night • and more.
00416928 Book only $6.99
00416929 Book/Audio $12.99

CHILDREN'S SONGS
arr. Carolyn Miller
MID-ELEMENTARY LEVEL
10 songs: The Candy Man • Do-Re-Mi • I'm Popeye the Sailor Man • It's a Small World • Linus and Lucy • The Muppet Show Theme • Sesame Street Theme • Supercalifragilisticexpialidocious • Tomorrow.
00416810 Book only $6.99
00416811 Book/Audio $12.99

CLASSICS
arr. Randall Hartsell
MID-ELEMENTARY LEVEL
7 solos: Marche Slave • Over the Waves • Polovtsian Dance (from the opera *Prince Igor*) • Pomp and Circumstance • Rondeau • Waltz (from the ballet *Sleeping Beauty*) • William Tell Overture.
00406760 Book only $5.99
00416513 Book/Audio $10.99

DISNEY TUNES
arr. Glenda Austin
MID-ELEMENTARY LEVEL
9 songs, including: Circle of Life • Colors of the Wind • A Dream Is a Wish Your Heart Makes • A Spoonful of Sugar • Under the Sea • A Whole New World • and more.
00416750 Book only $9.99
00416751 Book/Audio $12.99

EASY DUETS
arr. Carolyn Miller
MID-ELEMENTARY LEVEL
9 equal-level duets: A Bicycle Built for Two • Blow the Man Down • Chopsticks • Do Your Ears Hang Low? • I've Been Working on the Railroad • The Man on the Flying Trapeze • Short'nin' Bread • Skip to My Lou • The Yellow Rose of Texas.
00416832 Book only $6.99
00416833 Book/Audio $10.99

JAZZ AND ROCK
Eric Baumgartner
MID-ELEMENTARY LEVEL
11 solos, including: Big Bass Boogie • Crescendo Rock • Funky Fingers • Jazz Waltz in G • Rockin' Rhythm • Squirrel Race • and more!
00406765 Book only $5.99

MOVIE MUSIC
arr. Carolyn Miller
LATER ELEMENTARY LEVEL
10 magical movie arrangements: Bella's Lullaby (Twilight) • Somewhere Out There (An American Tail) • True Love's Kiss (Enchanted) • and more.
00139190 Book/Audio $10.99

Also available:

AMERICAN TUNES
arr. Eric Baumgartner
MID-ELEMENTARY LEVEL
00406755 Book only $6.99

BLUES AND BOOGIE
Carolyn Miller
MID-ELEMENTARY LEVEL
00406764 Book only $5.99

CHRISTMAS CAROLS
arr. Carolyn Miller
MID-ELEMENTARY LEVEL
00406763 Book only $6.99

CHRISTMAS CLASSICS
arr. Eric Baumgartner
MID-ELEMENTARY LEVEL
00416827 Book only $6.99
00416826 Book/Audio $12.99

CHRISTMAS FAVORITES
arr. Eric Baumgartner
MID-ELEMENTARY LEVEL
00416723 Book only $7.99
00416724 Book/Audio $12.99

FAMILIAR TUNES
arr. Glenda Austin
MID-ELEMENTARY LEVEL
00406761 Book only $6.99

HYMNS
arr. Glenda Austin
MID-ELEMENTARY LEVEL
00406762 Book only $6.99

JEWISH FAVORITES
arr. Eric Baumgartner
MID-ELEMENTARY LEVEL
00416755 Book only $5.99

RECITAL PIECES
Carolyn Miller
MID-ELEMENTARY LEVEL
00416540 Book only $5.99

SONGS FROM MANY LANDS
arr. Carolyn C. Setliff
MID-ELEMENTARY LEVEL
00416688 Book only $5.99

WILLIS MUSIC

EXCLUSIVELY DISTRIBUTED BY

HAL•LEONARD®

Complete song lists online at
www.halleonard.com